# BALLADS OF BOOKS

# BALLADS OF BOOKS

EDITED BY

ANDREW LANG

*Granger Index Reprint Series*

 BOOKS FOR LIBRARIES PRESS
FREEPORT, NEW YORK

First Published 1888
Reprinted 1969

TO

# FREDERICK LOCKER

POET AND LOVER OF BOOKS

'Come and take a choice of all my library'
Titus Andronicus, iv, 1

B. M.
A. L.

LIBRARY OF CONGRESS CATALOG CARD NUMBER:
75-75714

MANUFACTURED
BY
HALLMARK LITHOGRAPHERS, INC.
IN THE U.S.A.

# EDITOR'S PREFACE.

THIS collection, 'Ballads of Books,' is a recast of the volume of the same name, edited by Mr. Brander Matthews, and published by Mr. Coombes (New York, 1887). An editor must be meddling, and I have altered Mr. Matthews's work in some respects. The poems are now arranged by the dates of their authors, except where the moderns of to-day are all of much the same chronology. I have omitted some pieces, but all that were expressly written for Mr. Matthews's volume have been retained, and are marked with an asterisk in the Contents.

I have given some translations from Martial, from M. Fertiault, M. Boulmier, and the Swedish. These are by myself, and by Mr. Gosse and Mr. Graham R. Tomson. To Mr. Tomson I also am indebted for the 'Ballade of Biblioclasts.' A few pieces that had evaded Mr. Matthews have

been observed by myself or pointed out to me by
lovers of books.    The poems which cannot be
called lyrical are published separately, at the end.
Several rhymes of my own, which were in Mr.
Matthews's collection, I have struck out, as they
are printed in ' Books and Bookmen.'

It will not escape the reader that few very great
poets have written like bibliophiles, have been
lovers of books as *bibelots*.   But we may claim
Catullus, Horace, and Martial among the ancients,
as men who liked a book to be well appointed,
smooth of leaf, and adorned with red letters and
other delights.   Of the moderns, it is sure that
Scott and Southey had their hearts in the right
place ; how Wordsworth and Johnson treated the
bodies of books is over-well known.   Contempo-
raries have been copious in their songs of books,
few with so much earnestness as the late M. Joseph
Boulmier, whose old French ditty, as I cannot
translate it, I offer here in the original :—

### VNG LIVRE VIEL.

Vng livre viel m'arraisonnant tout bas,
Oncq n'ay congneu plus gente causerie.
De tel deuis si fay-je moult grand cas.
Vng livre viel m' arraisonnant tout bas,
Oncq n'ay congneu plus gente causerie

De luy respondre obligié ne suis pas ;
Puys, aduenant que i'entre en resuerie,
Lors il se taist sanz noyse n'altercas.
Vng livre viel m'arraisonnant tout bas,
Oncq n'ay congneu plus gente causerie.

Doubtless, bibliophiles who turn over this collection will miss some friends of whom one would be glad to hear. Perhaps some readers may be encouraged to become their own poets.

Mr. Matthews's dedication is preserved, and this English edition comes to a Poet and a Book-collector with good will from both the American and English Editors.

# PREFATORY NOTE.

———◆◇◆———

THE poets have ever been lovers of books ; indeed,
one might ask how should a man be a poet who
did not admire a treasure as precious and as beautiful as a book may be.    With evident enjoyment,
Keats describes

> A viol, bowstrings torn, cross-wise upon
> A glorious folio of Anacreon ;

and it was a glorious folio of Beaumont and Fletcher
which another English poet (whose most poetic
work was done in prose) 'dragged home late at
night from Barker's in Covent Garden,' and to
pacify his conscience for the purchase of which he
kept to his over-worn suit of clothes for four or five
weeks longer than he ought.    Charles Lamb was
a true bibliophile, in the earlier and more exact
sense of the term ; he loved his ragged volumes as
he loved his fellow-men, and he was as intolerant

of books that are not books as he was of men who
were not manly.    He conferred the dukedom of
his library on Coleridge, who was no respecter of
books, though he could not but enrich them with
his marginal notes.    Southey and Lord Houghton
and Mr. Locker are English poets with libraries
of their own, more orderly and far richer than the
fortuitous congregation of printed atoms, a mere
medley of unrelated tomes, which often mas-
querades as The Library in the mansions of the
noble and the wealthy.    Shelley said that he thought
Southey had a secret in every one of his books
which he was afraid the stranger might discover :
but this was probably no more, and no other, than
the secret of comfort, consolation, refreshment, and
happiness to be found in any library by him who
shall bring with him the golden key that unlocks
its silent door.

Mr. Lowell has recently dwelt on the difference
between literature and books : and, accepting this
distinction, the editor desires to declare at once
that as a whole this collection is devoted rather to
books than to literature.    The poems in the follow-
ing pages celebrate the bric-à-brac of the one
rather than the masterpieces of the other.    The
stanzas here garnered into one sheaf sing of books

as books, of books valuable and valued for their perfection of type and page and printing,—for their beauty and for their rarity,—or for their association with some famous man or woman of the storied past.

Two centuries and a half ago Drummond of Hawthornden prefixed to the 'Varieties' of his friend Persons a braggart distich :—

> This book a world is ; here, if errors be,
> The like, nay worse, in the great world we see.

The present collection of varieties in verse has little or naught to do with the great world and its errors : it has to do chiefly, not to say wholly, with the world of the Bookmen—the little world of the Book-lover, the Bibliophile, the Bibliomaniac—a mad world, my masters, in which there are to be found not a few poets who cherish old wine and old wood, old friends and old books, and who believe that old books are the best of old friends.

> Books, books again, and books once more !
> These are our theme, which some miscall
> Mere madness, setting little store
> By copies either short or tall.
> But you, O slaves of shelf and stall !
> We rather write for you that hold
> Patched folios dear, and prize 'the small
> Rare volume, black with burnished gold.'

as Mr. Austin Dobson sang on the threshold of
Mr. Lang's book about the ' Library.'

The editor has much pleasure in thanking the
poets who have allowed him to reprint their poems
in these pages ; and he acknowledges a double
debt of gratitude to the friends who have written
poems expressly for this collection. Encouraged
by their support, and remembering that he is not
a contributor to his own pages, the editor ventures
to conclude his harmless necessary catalogue of
the things contained and not contained within
these covers, by quoting Herrick's address to his
Book :—

> Be bold, my Book, nor be abash'd, or fear,
> The cutting thumb-nail, or the brow severe ;
> But by the muses swear, all here is good,
> If but well read, or ill read, understood.

BRANDER MATTHEWS.

NEW YORK, *November*, 1886.

# CONTENTS.

Pieces marked * were written or translated for this collection.

## PROEM.

### BALLADE OF THE BOOKWORM.

*Far in the Past I peer, and see*
*A Child upon the Nursery floor,*
*A Child with book, upon his knee,*
*Who asks, like Oliver, for more !*
*The number of his years is IV,*
*And yet in Letters hath he skill,*
*How deep he dives in Fairy-lore !*
*The Books I loved, I love them still !*

*One gift the Fairies gave me : (Three*
*They commonly bestowed of yore)*
*The Love of Books, the Golden Key*
*That opens the Enchanted Door ;*
*Behind it BLUEBEARD lurks and o'er*
*And o'er doth JACK his Giants kill,*
*And there is all ALADDIN'S store,—*
*The Books I loved, I love them still !*

*Take all, but leave my Books to me !*
*These heavy creels of old we bore*
*We fill not now, nor wander free,*
*Nor wear the heart that once we wore ;*

*Not now each River seems to pour*
*His waters from the Muse's hill;*
*Though something's gone from stream and shore,*
*The Books I loved, I love them still!*

*ENVOY!*

*Fate, that art Queen by shore and sea,*
*We bow submissive to thy will,*
*Ah grant, by some benign decree,*
*The Books I loved—to love them still.*

A. LANG.

# BALLADS OF BOOKS.

—◆—

## CATULLUS TO HIS BOOK.

### QVOI DONO LEPIDVM NOVVM LIBELLVM.

CAIUS VALERIUS CATULLUS.

M Y little book, that's neat and new,
  Fresh polished with dry pumice stone,
To whom, Cornelius, but to you,
Shall *this* be sent, for you alone—
(Who used to praise my lines, my own)—
Have dared, in weighty volumes three,
(What labours, Jove, what learning thine !)
To tell the Tale of Italy,
And all the legend of our line.

So take, whate'er its worth may be,
My Book,—but Lady and Queen of Song,
This one kind gift I crave of thee,
That it may live for ages long !

                                   A. L.

## TO HIS BOOK.

HORACE.                                   *Epist. i.* 20.

FOR mart and street you seem to pine
    With restless glances, Book of mine !
Still craving on some stall to stand,
Fresh pumiced from the binder's hand.
You chafe at locks, and burn to quit
Your modest haunt and audience fit,
For hearers less discriminate.
I reared you up for no such fate.
Still, if you *must* be published, go ;
But mind, you can't come back, you know !

'What have I done ? '—I hear you cry,
And writhe beneath some critic's eye ;
'What did I want ? '—when, scarce polite,
They do but yawn, and roll you tight.
And yet, methinks, if I may guess
(Putting aside your heartlessness
In leaving me, and this your home),
You should find favour, too, at Rome.
That is, they'll like you while you're young.
When you are old, you'll pass among

The Great Unwashed,—then thumbed and sped,
Be fretted of slow moths, unread,
Or to Ilerda you'll be sent,
Or Utica, for banishment !
And I, whose counsel you disdain,
At that your lot shall laugh amain,
Wryly, as he who, like a fool,
Pushed o'er the cliff his restive mule.
Nay, there is worse behind.   In age
They e'en may take your babbling page
In some remotest 'slum' to teach
Mere boys the rudiments of speech !
But go.   When on warm days you see
A chance of listeners, speak of me.
Tell them I soared from low estate,
A freedman's son, to higher fate
(That is, make up to me in worth
What you must take in point of birth) ;
Then tell them that I won renown
In peace and war, and pleased the Town ;
Paint me as early gray, and one
Little of stature, fond of sun,
Quick-tempered, too,—but nothing more.
Add (if they ask) I'm forty-four,
Or was, the year that over us
Both Lollius ruled and Lepidus.

A. D.

## THE STINGY FRIEND.

MARTIAL.                                   *cxviii.*

YOU cry, whene'er you meet me still,
      'I'll send my boy, an' if you will,
To whom perhaps you'll kindly lend
Your *Epigrams*, and these, my friend,
I'll send you, when I've read them through.'
No need, good sir, no need that you
Should tire your boy ; 'tis far and high,
My three-pair garret, near the sky.
And, for my books, at hand you'll meet 'em.
You often stroll in Argiletum?
Well, there you'll find a shop in face
Of the Imperial Marketplace.
The new books' names are on the doors,
And poets may be read in scores.
There ask Attrectus—that is he
Who keeps the shop—to sell you *me*.
He'll give, from first or second shelf—
Polished and purple-clad—myself!
*Martial* for fivepence !   ' Dear, in sooth ! '
Perhaps, my friend, you speak the truth.

                                   A. L.

## HIS BOOK'S PATRON.

MARTIAL. *iii.* 2.

TO whom shalt Thou be dedicate?
　　Get thee a patron e'er it's late—
My Book—ere thou, without a friend,
Into the kitchen's deeps descend,
To wrap up spices for the pot,
Or shroud a fish *en papillotte* !

Faustinus ! Him for friend you've found?
Wise book that shalt go bravely bound,
Fragrant, with painted bosses graced,
In dainty purple all embraced,
And with red title-page ! My Book,
Fear neither Critics nor the Cook !

　　　　　　　　　　A. L.

## HIS BOOKSELLER'S ADDRESS.

MARTIAL.　　　　　　　　　　　　　　　　　*i. 2.*

YOU that would have my books to fare
　　Companions with you everywhere,
Buy *these* that but one hand engage,
In parchment bound, with tiny page.
Your desks, your scaffoldings, bestow
On some majestic folio !

My books you'll buy—no need that you
The whole wide town should wander through.—
Where one Secundus lives apart,
Behind the fane of Peace, the Mart
Palladian—he my books that sells,
Lucensis' freedman—*there* he dwells.

　　　　　　　　　　　　　　A. L.

## VIRGIL.

MARTIAL.                                          *xiv*. 86.

GREAT Virgil this small parchment book enfolds ;
Its opening leaf his painted portrait holds.

E. G.

## CICERO.

88.

If on a journey with this book you go,
Your fellow-traveller will be Cicero.

E. G.

## CONCERNING THE HONOUR OF BOOKS.

SAMUEL DANIEL.

*This sonnet, prefixed to the second edition of Florio's Montaigne, 1613, is generally attributed to the translator, but the best critics now incline to the belief that it is by his friend, Daniel.*

SINCE honour from the honourer proceeds,
   How well do they deserve, that memorise
And leave in books for all posterities
The names of worthies, and their virtuous deeds ;
When all their glory else, like water-weeds
Without their element, presently dies,
And all their greatness quite forgotten lies,
And when and how they flourisht no man heeds ;
How poor remembrances are statues, tombs,
And other monuments that men erect
To Princes, which remain in closèd rooms,
Where but a few behold them, in respect
Of books, that to the universal eye
Show how they lived ; the other where they lie !

## TO HIS BOOK. OF HIS LADY.

EDMUND SPENSER.                                                    *Amoretti, i.*

HAPPY, ye leaves ! when as those lilly hands,
  Which hold my life in their dead-doing might,
Shall handle you, and hold in love's soft bands,
Lyke captives trembling at the victors sight.
And happy lines ! on which, with starry light,
Those lamping eyes will deigne sometimes to looke,
And reade the sorrowes of my dying spright,
Written with teares in harts close-bleeding booke.
And happy rymes ! bath'd in the sacred brooke
Of Helicon, whence she derived is ;
When ye behold that Angels blessed looke,
My soules long-lacked foode, my heavens blis ;
    Leaves, lines, and rymes, seeke her to please alone,
    Whom if ye please, I care for other none !

## TO MY BOOKSELLER.

BEN JONSON.

*This is from the third of the poet's books of epigrams. Bucklersbury was the street most affected by grocers and apothecaries.*

THOU that mak'st gain thy end, and wisely well,
 Call'st a book good, or bad, as it doth sell,
Use mine so, too ; I give thee leave.   But crave,
For the luck's sake, it thus much favour have,
To lie upon thy stall, till it be sought ;
Not offered, as it made suit to be bought ;
Nor have my title-leaf on posts, or walls,
Or in cleft-sticks, advanced to make calls
For termers, or some clerk-like serving-man,
Who scarce can spell th' hard names ; whose knight less
 can.
If without these vile arts, it will not sell,
Send it to Bucklersbury, there 'twill well.

## TO SIR HENRY GOODYERE.

BEN JONSON.

*This is the eighty-sixth of the poet's first book of epigrams, and, like its immediate predecessor, it was addressed to a gentleman bound in bonds of friendship to many of the men of genius of his time.*

WHEN I would know thee, Goodyere, my thought
      looks
Upon thy well-made choice of friends, and books ;
Then do I love thee, and behold thy ends
In making thy friends books, and thy books friends :
Now must I give thy life and deed the voice
Attending such a study, such a choice ;
Where, though 't be love that to thy praise doth move,
It was a knowledge that begat that love.

## TO HIS BOOKE.

ROBERT HERRICK.                    *Prefixed to ' Hesperides.'*  1648.

WHILE thou didst keep thy Candor undefil'd,
  Deerely I lov'd thee ; as my first-borne child :
But when I saw thee wantonly to roame
From house to house, and never stay at home ;
I brake my bonds of Love, and bad thee goe,
Regardlesse whether well thou sped'st, or no.
On with thy fortunes then, whate'er they be ;
If good I'le smile, if bad I'le sigh for Thee.

## HIS POETS.

ROBERT HERRICK. *Hesperides, p.* 88.

NOW is the time for mirth,
　　Nor cheek, or tongue be dumbe;
For with flowrie earth,
　　The golden pomp is come.

The golden Pomp is come ;
　　For now each tree do's weare
(Made of her Pap and Gum)
　　Rich beads of *Amber* here.

Now raignes the *Rose,* and now
　　Th' *Arabian* Dew besmears
My uncontrollèd brow,
　　And my retorted haires.

*Homer,* this health to thee,
　　In Sack of such a kind,
That it wo'd make thee see,
　　Though thou wert ne'r so blind.

Next, *Virgil*, I'le call forth,
　To pledge this second Health
In Wine, whose each cup's worth
　An Indian Common-wealth.

A Goblet next I'le drink
　To *Ovid*; and suppose,
Made he the pledge, he'd think
　The world had all *one Nose*.

Then this immensive cup
　Of *Aromatike* wine,
*Catullus*, I quaffe up
　To that Terce Muse of thine.

Wild am I now with heat ;
　O *Bacchus* ! coole thy Raies !
Or frantick I shall eat
　Thy *Thyrse*, and bite the *Bayes*.

Round, round, the roof do's run ;
　And being ravisht thus,
Come, I will drink a tun
　To my *Propertius*.

Now to *Tibullus*, next,
　This flood I drink to thee :
But stay ; I see a Text,
　That this presents to me.

Behold, *Tibullus* lies
　　Here burnt, whose smal return
Of ashes, scarce suffice
　　To fill a little Urne.

Trust to good Verses then ;
　　They onely will aspire,
When Pyramids, as men,
　　Are lost, i' th' funerall fire.

And when all Bodies meet
　　In *Lethe* to be drowned ;
Then onely Numbers sweet,
　　With endless life are crowned.

## TO HIS BOOK.

ROBERT HERRICK.

MAKE haste away, and let one be
    A friendly Patron unto thee ;
Lest rapt from hence, I see thee lye
Torn for the use of Pasterie ;
Or see thy injur'd Leaves serve well,
To make loose Gownes for Mackerell :
Or see the Grocers in a trice,
Make hoods of thee to serve out Spice.

## TO HIS BOOKS.

HENRY VAUGHAN.     *From ' Silex Scintillans : Sacred Poems and Pious Ejaculations.' 1678.*

BRIGHT books : perspectives on our weak sights,
  The clear projections of discerning lights,
Burning in shining thoughts, man's posthume day,
The track of fled souls in their milkie way,
The dead alive and busy, the still voice
Of enlarged spirits, kind heaven's white decoys !
Who lives with you lives like those knowing flowers
Which in commerce with light spend all their hours ;
Which shut to clouds, and shadows nicely shun,
But with glad haste unveil to kiss the sun.
Beneath you all is dark and a dead night,
Which whoso lives in wants both health and sight.
By sucking you, the wise, like bees, do grow
Healing and rich, though this they do most slow,
Because most choicely ; for as great a store
Have we of books as bees, of herbs, or more ;
And the great task to try, then know, the good,
To discern weeds, and judge of wholesome food,
Is a rare scant performance.   For man dies

Oft ere 'tis done, while the bee feeds and flies.
But you were all choice flowers ; all set and drest
By old sage florists, who well knew the best ;
And I amidst you all am turned to weed !
Not wanting knowledge, but for want of heed.
Then thank thyself, wild fool, that would'st not be
Content to know what was too much for thee !

## THE BOOKWORM.

THOMAS PARNELL.                    *Translated from the Latin of*
                                   *Theodore Beza.*

COME hither, boy, we'll hunt to day
     The bookworm, ravening beast of prey,
Produc'd by parent Earth, at odds,
As fame reports it, with the gods.
Him frantic hunger wildly drives
Against a thousand authors' lives :
Through all the fields of wit he flies ;
Dreadful his head with clustering eyes,
With horns without, and tusks within,
And scales to serve him for a skin.
Observe him nearly, lest he climb
To wound the bards of ancien  time,
Or down the vale of fancy go
To tear some modern wretch below.
On every corner fix thine eye,
Or ten to one he slips thee by.

See where his teeth a passage eat :
We'll rouse him from his deep retreat.
But who the shelter 's forc'd to give ?

'Tis sacred Virgil, as I live !
From leaf to leaf, from song to song
He draws the tadpole form along,
He mounts the gilded edge before,
He's up, he scuds the cover o'er,
He turns, he doubles, there he past,
And here we have him, caught at last.

Insatiate brute, whose teeth abuse
The sweetest servants of the Muse—
Nay, never offer to deny,
I took thee in the fact to fly.
His roses nipt in every page,
My poor Anacreon mourns thy rage ;
By thee my Ovid wounded lies ;
By thee my Lesbia's Sparrow dies ;
Thy rabid teeth have half destroy'd
The work of love in Biddy Floyd ;
They rent Belinda's locks away,
And spoil'd the Blouzelind of Gay.
For all, for every single deed,
Relentless justice bids thee bleed :
Then fall a victim to the Nine,
Myself the priest, my desk the shrine.

Bring Homer, Virgil, Tasso near,
To pile a sacred altar here :

Hold, boy, thy hand outruns thy wit,
You reach'd the plays that Dennis writ ;
You reach'd me Philips' rustic strain ;
Pray take your mortal bards again.

Come, bind the victim,—there he lies,
And here between his numerous eyes
This venerable dust I lay
From manuscripts just swept away.
The goblet in my hand I take,
For the libation 's yet to make :
A health to poets ! all their days
May they have bread, as well as praise ;
Sense may they seek, and less engage
In papers fill'd with party rage.
But if their riches spoil their vein,
Ye Muses, make them poor again.

Now bring the weapon, yonder blade
With which my tuneful pens are made.
I strike the scales that arm thee round,
And twice and thrice I print the wound;
The sacred altar floats with red,
And now he dies, and now he's dead.

How like the son of Jove I stand,
This Hydra stretch'd beneath the hand !
Lay bare the monster's entrails here,

And see what dangers threat the year :
Ye gods ! what sonnets on a wench !
What lean translations out of French !
'Tis plain, this lobe is so unsound,
S—prints, before the months go round.

But hold, before I close the scene
The sacred altar should be clean.
O had I Shadwell's second bays,
Or, Tate, thy pert and humble lays !
(Ye pair, forgive me, when I vow
I never miss'd your works till now,)
I'd tear the leaves to wipe the shrine,
That only way you please the Nine :
But since I chance to want these two,
I'll make the songs of Durfey do.

Rent from the corpse, on yonder pin,
I hang the scales that brac'd it in ;
I hang my studious morning gown,
And write my own inscription down.

' This trophy from the Python won,
This robe, in which the deed was done,
These, Parnell, glorying in the feat
Hung on these shelves, the Muses' seat.
Here Ignorance and Hunger found

Large realms of wit to ravage round ;
Here Ignorance and Hunger fell
Two foes in one I sent to hell.
Ye poets who my labours see
Come share the triumph all with me !
Ye critics, born to vex the Muse,
Go mourn the grand ally you lose !

## THE BOOKWORMS.

ROBERT BURNS.

*Burns saw a splendidly bound but sadly neglected copy of Shakspere in the library of a nobleman in Edinburgh, and he wrote these lines on the ample margin of one of its pages, where they were found long after the poet's death.*

THROUGH and through the inspired leaves,
　　Ye maggots, make your windings ;
But oh, respect his lordship's taste,
　　And spare the golden bindings.

## ONE VOLUME MORE.

SIR WALTER SCOTT. 1823. *Poetical Works*, 1833, *vol. xi.*

ASSIST me, ye friends of Old Books and Old Wine,
 To sing in the praises of sage Bannatyne,
Who left such a treasure of old Scottish lore
As enables each age to print one volume more.
 One volume more, my friends, one volume more,
 We'll ransack old Banny for one volume more.

And first, Allan Ramsay was eager to glean
From Bannatyne's *Hortus* his bright *Evergreen* ;
Two light little volumes (intended for four)
Still leave us the task to print one volume more.

His ways were not ours, for he cared not a pin
How much he left out, or how much he put in;
The truth of the reading he thought was a bore,
So this accurate age calls for one volume more.

Correct and sagacious then came my Lord Hailes,
And weighed every letter in critical scales,
But left out some brief words, which the prudish abhor,
And castrated Banny in one volume more.

John Pinkerton next, and I'm truly concern'd
I can't call that worthy so candid as learn'd,
He rail'd at the plaid and blasphemed the claymore,
And set Scots by the ears in his one volume more.

As bitter as gall, and as sharp as a razor,
And feeding on herbs like a Nebuchadnezzar ;
His diet too acid, his temper too sour,
Little Ritson came out with his one volume more.

The stout Gothic Yeditur,[1] next on the roll,
With his beard like a brush, and as black as a coal ;
And honest Greysteel,[2] that was true to the core,
Lent their hearts and their hands each to one volume
    more.

Since by these single champions what wonders were
    done,
What may not be achieved by our Thirty and One ?
Law, Gospel, and Commerce, we count in our corps,
And the Trade and the Press join for one volume
    more.

Ancient libels and contraband books, I assure ye,
We'll print as secure from Exchequer or Jury;
Then hear your Committee and let them count o'er
The Chiels they intend in their three volumes more.

[1] James Sibbald.              [2] David Herd.

They'll produce you King Jamie, the sapient and sext,
And the Rob of Dumblane and her bishops come
  next ;
One tome miscellaneous they'll add to your store,
Resolving next year to print four volumes more.

  Four volumes more, my friends, four volumes more,
  Pay down your subscriptions for four volumes more.[1]

---

[1] George Bannatyne, whose MSS. were reprinted under Sir Walter's presidency of the Bannatyne Club, was a scholar who, in 1568, copied out a quantity of perishing books, especially of Old Scotch poetry. This task beguiled him in a time of pestilence.

# THE LIBRARY.

ROBERT SOUTHEY.                    *Written at Keswick in* 1818.

MY days among the Dead are past ;
    Around me I behold,
Where'er these casual eyes are cast,
    The mighty minds of old ;
My never-failing friends are they,
With whom I converse day by day.

With them I take delight in weal,
    And seek relief in woe ;
And while I understand and feel
    How much to them I owe,
My cheeks have often been bedew'd
With tears of thoughtful gratitude.

My thoughts are with the Dead, with them
    I live in long-past years,
Their virtues love, their faults condemn ;
    Partake their hopes and fears,
And from their lessons seek and find
Instruction with an humble mind.

My hopes are with the Dead, anon
   My place with them shall be,
And I with them shall travel on
   Through all futurity ;
Yet leaving here a name, I trust,
That will not perish in the dust.

## IN THE ALBUM OF LUCY BARTON.

CHARLES LAMB.                    *Written in 1824 for the daughter of his friend Bernard Barton.*

L ITTLE Book, surnamed of *white*,
      Clean as yet and fair to sight,
Keep thy attribution right.

Never disproportioned scrawl ;
Ugly blot, that's worse than all ;
On thy maiden clearness fall !

In each letter, here designed,
Let the reader emblemed find
Neatness of the owner's mind.

Gilded margins count a sin,
Let thy leaves attraction win
By the golden rules within ;

Sayings fetched from sages old ;
Laws which Holy Writ unfold,
Worthy to be graved in gold :

Lighter fancies not excluding ;
Blameless wit, with nothing rude in,
Sometimes mildly interluding,

Amid strains of graver measure :
Virtue's self hath oft her pleasure
In sweet Muses' groves of leisure.

Riddles dark, perplexing sense ;
Darker meanings of offence ;
What but *shades*—be banished hence.

Whitest thoughts in whitest dress,
Candid meanings, best express
Mind of quiet Quakeress.

## MY BOOKS.

BRYAN WALLER PROCTER
(BARRY CORNWALL).                    *From 'An Autobiographical
                    Fragment,' 1877.*

ALL round the room my silent servants wait,—
    My friends in every season, bright and dim ;
Angels and seraphim
Come down and murmur to me, sweet and low,
And spirits of the skies all come and go
Early and late ;
All from the old world's divine and distant date,
From the sublimer few,
Down to the poet who but yester-eve
Sang sweet and made us grieve,
All come, assembling here in order due.
And here I dwell with Poesy, my mate,
With Erato and all her vernal sighs,
Great Clio with her victories elate,
Or pale Urania's deep and starry eyes.

O friends, whom chance and change can never harm,
Whom Death the tyrant cannot doom to die,
Within whose folding soft eternal charm
I love to lie,
And meditate upon your verse that flows,
And fertilises whereso'er it goes,
Whether. . . . .

## TO MY BOOKS ON PARTING WITH THEM.

WILLIAM ROSCOE.            *The sale of the famous Roscoe Library,*
                          *made necessary by reverses in business,*
                          *took place in August and September,* 1816.

A S one who, destined from his friends to part,
    Regrets his loss, yet hopes again erewhile,
To share their converse and enjoy their smile,
And tempers as he may affliction's dart,—
Thus, loved associates ! chiefs of elder Art !
Teachers of wisdom ! who could once beguile
My tedious hours, and lighten every toil,
I now resign you ; nor with fainting heart ;
For pass a few short years, or days, or hours
And happier seasons may their dawn unfold,
And all your sacred fellowship restore ;
When, freed from earth, unlimited its powers,
Mind shall with mind direct communion hold,
And kindred spirits meet to part no more.

## HIS POETS.

*Found by Mr. Alexander Ireland in the London 'Examiner' of December 24, 1815, and not anywhere included in the poet's collected works.*

LEIGH HUNT.

WERE I to name, out of the times gone by,
    The poets dearest to me, I should say,
Pulci for spirits, and a fine, free way ;
Chaucer for manners, and close, silent eye ;
Milton for classic taste, and harp strung high ;
Spenser for luxury, and sweet, sylvan play ;
Horace for chatting with, from day to day ;
Shakspere for all, but most—society.

But which take with me, could I take but one ?
Shakspere, as long as I was unoppressed
With the world's weight, making sad thoughts intenser ;
But did I wish, out of the common sun,
To lay a wounded heart in leafy rest,
And dream of things far off and healing,—Spenser.

## THE BOOK OF LIFE.

RICHARD THOMSON.  *A Bibliographical Melody, printed in* 1820
*at the press of John Johnson, as a gift
to the members of the Roxburghe Club.*

THAT Life is a Comedy oft hath been shown,
　　By all who Mortality's changes have known ;
But more like a Volume its actions appear,
Where each Day is a Page and each Chapter a year.
'Tis a Manuscript Time shall full surely unfold,
Though with Black-Letter shaded, or shining with gold ;
The Initial, like Youth, glitters bright on its Page,
But its Text is as dark—as the gloom of Old Age.
　　Then Life's Counsels of Wisdom engrave on thy breast,
　　And deep on thine Heart be her lessons imprest.

Though the Title stands first it can little declare
The Contents which the Pages ensuing shall bear ;
As little the first day of Life can explain
The succeeding events which shall glide in its train.
The Book follows next, and, delighted, we trace
An Elzevir's beauty, a Gutenberg's grace ;

Thus on pleasure we gaze with as raptured an eye,
Till, cut off like a Volume imperfect, we die !
    Then Life's Counsels of Wisdom engrave on thy breast,
    And deep on thine Heart be her lessons imprest.

Yet e'en thus imperfect, complete, or defaced,
The skill of the Printer is still to be traced ;
And though death bend us early in life to his will,
The wise hand of our Author is visible still.
Like the Colophon lines is the Epitaph's lay,
Which tells of what age and what nation our day,
And, like the Device of the Printer, we bear
The form of the Founder, whose Image we wear.
    Then Life's Counsels of Wisdom engrave on thy breast,
    And deep on thine Heart be her lessons imprest.

The work thus completed its Boards shall inclose,
Till a Binding more bright and more beauteous it shows ;
And who can deny, when Life's Vision hath past,
That the dark Boards of Death shall surround us at last.
Yet our Volume illumed with fresh splendours shall rise,
To be gazed at by Angels, and read to the skies,
Reviewed by its Author, revised by his Pen,
In a fair new Edition to flourish again.
    Then Life's Counsels of Wisdom engrave on thy breast,
    And deep on thine Heart be her lessons imprest.

# THE BORROWED BOOK.

CHARLES NODIER.

TEL est le triste sort de tout livre prêté,
  Souvent il est perdu, toujours il est gâté !

Such is the fate of borrowed Books : they're lost,
Or not the Book returneth, but its Ghost !

## OVER THE THRESHOLD OF MY LIBRARY.

HENRY DRURY.

*Quoted from the supplement of Dibdin's 'Bibliomania,' where the original Latin lines may be found.*

FROM mouldering Abbey's dark Scriptorium brought,
　　See vellum tomes by Monkish labour wrought ;
Nor yet the comma born, Papyri see,
And uncial letters' wizard grammary ;
View my *fifteeners* in their ragged line ;
What ink !　What linen !　Only known long syne—
Entering where Aldus might have fixed his throne,
Or Harry Stephens coveted his own.

## ON CERTAIN BOOKS.

CHARLES TENNYSON TURNER.              *From 'Sonnets.'* 1864.

FAITH and fixt hope these pages may peruse,
    And still be faith and hope ; but, O ye winds !
Blow them far off from all unstable minds,
And foolish grasping hands of youth !   Ye dews
Of heaven ! be pleased to rot them where they fall,
Lest loitering boys their fancies should abuse,
And they get harm by chance, that cannot choose ;
So be they stain'd and sodden, each and all !
And if, perforce, on dry and gusty days,
Upon the breeze some truant leaf should rise,
Brittle with many weathers, to the skies,
Or flit and dodge about the public ways—
Man's choral shout, or organ's peal of praise
Shall shake it into dust, like older lies.

## MY BOOKS.

WILLIS FLETCHER JOHNSON.                    *From the Boston ' Transcript.'*

ON my study shelves they stand,
 Well known all to eye and hand,
Bound in gorgeous cloth of gold,
In morocco rich and old.
Some in paper, plain and cheap,
Some in muslin, calf, and sheep ;
Volumes great and volumes small,
Ranged along my study wall ;
But their contents are past finding
By their size or by their binding.

There is one with gold agleam,
Like the Sangreal in a dream,
Back and boards in every part
Triumph of the binder's art ;
Costing more, 'tis well believed,
Than the author e'er received.
But its contents ?   Idle tales,
Flappings of a shallop's sails !
In the treasury of learning
Scarcely worth a penny's turning.

Here's a tome in paper plain,
Soiled and torn and marred with stain,
Cowering from each statelier book
In the darkest, dustiest nook.
Take it down, and lo ! each page
Breathes the wisdom of a sage :
Weighed a thousand times in gold,
Half its worth would not be told,
For all truth of ancient story
Crowns each line with deathless glory.

On my study shelves they stand ;
But my study walls expand,
As thought's pinions are unfurled,
Till they compass all the world.
Endless files go marching by,
Men of lowly rank and high,
Some in broadcloth, gem-adorned,
Some in homespun, fortune-scorned ;
But God's scales that all are weighed in
Heed not what each man's arrayed in !

## MY BOOKS.

AUSTIN DOBSON.                    *From 'At the Sign of the Lyre.'* 1885.

THEY dwell in the odour of camphor,
  They stand in a Sheraton shrine,
They are 'warranted early editions,'
  These worshipful tomes of mine ;—

In their creamy 'Oxford vellum,'
  In their redolent 'crushed Levant,'
With their delicate watered linings,
  They are jewels of price, I grant ;—

Blind-tooled and morocco-jointed,
  They have Bedford's daintiest dress,
They are graceful, attenuate, polished,
  But they gather the dust, no less ;—

For the row that I prize is yonder,
  Away on the unglazed shelves,
The bulged and the bruised *octavos*,
  The dear and the dumpy twelves,—

Montaigne with his sheepskin blistered,
　And Howell the worse for wear,
And the worm-drilled Jesuits' Horace,
　And the little old cropped Molière,—

And the Burton I bought for a florin,
　And the Rabelais foxed and flea'd,—
For the others I never have opened,
　But those are the ones I read.

## TO A MISSAL OF THE THIRTEENTH CENTURY.

AUSTIN DOBSON.                    *From ' At the Sign of the Lyre.'* 1885.

M ISSAL of the Gothic age,
  Missal with the blazoned page,
Whence, O Missal, hither come,
From what dim Scriptorium ?

Whose the name that wrought thee thus,
Ambrose or Theophilus,
Bending, through the waning light,
O'er thy vellum scraped and white ;

Weaving 'twixt thy rubric lines
Sprays and leaves and quaint designs ;
Setting round thy border scrolled
Buds of purple and of gold ?

Ah !—a wondering brotherhood,
Doubtless, by that artist stood,
Raising o'er his careful ways
Little choruses of praise ;

Glad when his deft hand would paint
Strife of Sathanas and Saint,
Or in secret coign entwist
Jest of cloister humorist.

Well the worker earned his wage,
Bending o'er the blazoned page !
Tired the hand and tired the wit
Ere the final *Explicit* !

Not as ours the books of old—
Things that steam can stamp and fold ;
Not as ours the books of yore—
Rows of type, and nothing more.

Then a book was still a Book,
Where a wistful man might look,
Finding something through the whole,
Beating—like a human soul.

In that growth of day by day,
When to labour was to pray,
Surely something vital passed
To the patient page at last ;

Something that one still perceives
Vaguely present in the leaves ;
Something from the worker lent ;
Something mute—but eloquent !

## THE BOOK-PLATE'S PETITION.

### BY A GENTLEMAN OF THE TEMPLE.

AUSTIN DOBSON.                 *Published originally in ' Notes and
Queries,' January* 8, 1881.

W HILE cynic CHARLES still trimm'd the vane
    'Twixt *Querouaille* and *Castlemaine,*
In days that shocked JOHN EVELYN,
My First Possessor fix'd me in.
In days of *Dutchmen* and of frost,
The narrow sea with JAMES I crossed,
Returning when once more began
The Age of *Saturn* and of ANNE.
I am a part of all the past ;
I knew the GEORGES, first and last ;
I have been oft where else was none
Save the great wig of ADDISON ;
And seen on shelves beneath me grope
The little eager form of POPE.
I lost the Third that own'd me when
French NOAILLES fled at Dettingen ;
The year JAMES WOLFE surpris'd Quebec,
The Fourth in hunting broke his neck ;

The day that WILLIAM HOGARTH dy'd,
The Fifth one found me in Cheapside.
This was a *Scholar*, one of those
Whose *Greek* is sounder than their *hose* ;
He lov'd old books, and nappy ale,
So liv'd at Streatham, next to THRALE.
'Twas there this stain of grease I boast
Was made by DR. JOHNSON's toast.
(He did it, as I think, for spite ;
My Master called him *Jacobite !*)
And now that I so long to-day
Have rested *post discrimina,*
Safe in the brass-wir'd book-case where
I watched the Vicar's whit'ning hair,
Must I these travell'd bones inter
In some *Collector's* sepulchre !
Must I be torn from hence and thrown
With *frontispiece* and *colophon !*
With vagrant *E*'s, and *I*'s and *O*'s,
The spoil of plunder'd *Folios !*
With scraps and snippets that to Me
Are naught but *kitchen company !*
Nay, rather, Friend, this favour grant me ;
Tear me at once ; *but don't transplant me.*

CHELTENHAM,
     *Sept.* 31, 1792.

## A RUINED LIBRARY.

WALTER HERRIES POLLOCK.        *Written for the present collection.*

' IMPERIOUS Cæsar dead and turn'd to clay
    Might stop a hole to keep the wind away.'
Here the live thought of buried Cæsar's brain
Has served a lazy slut to lay the train
That lights a dunce's fire.   Here Homer's seen
All torn or crumpled in the pettish spleen
Of some spoilt urchin.   Here a leaf from Glanvil
Is reft to mark a place in ' On the Anvil.'
Here, too, a heavy-blotted Shakspere's page
Holds up an inky mirror to the age ;
Here looking round you're but too sure to see a
Heart-breaking wreck from the ' Via Jacobæa ; '
Here some rare pamphlet, long a-missing, lurks
In an odd volume of ' Lord Bacon's Works ; '
Here may you find a Stillingfleet or Blair
Usurp the binding of a lost Voltaire ;
And here a tattered Boyle doth gape ungently
Upon a damp-disfigured ' Life of Bentley.'

Here half a Rabelais jostles for position
The quarter of a ' Spanish Inquisition ; '
Here Young's ' Night Thoughts' lie mixed with Swin-
 burne's ' Ballads'
'Mid scraps of works on Poisons and on Salads ;
And here a rent and gilt-edged Sterne doth lack a ray
Of sun that falls upon a bulging Thackeray ;
Here—but the tale's too sad at length to tell
How a book-heaven 's been turned to a book-hell.

## THE ART OF BOOK-KEEPING.

LAMAN BLANCHARD.          *From his 'Poetical Works.'* 1876.

HOW hard, when those who do not wish
  To lend, that's lose, their books,
Are snared by anglers—folks that fish
  With literary hooks ;

Who call and take some favourite tome,
  But never read it through,—
They thus complete their set at home,
  By making one at you.

Behold the bookshelf of a dunce
  Who borrows—never lends :
Yon work, in twenty volumes, once
  Belonged to twenty friends.

New tales and novels you may shut
  From view—'tis all in vain ;
They're gone—and though the leaves are 'cut'
  They never 'come again.'

For pamphlets lent I look around,
    For tracts my tears are spilt ;
But when they take a book that's bound,
    'Tis surely extra-gilt.

A circulating library
    Is mine—my birds are flown ;
There's one odd volume left to be
    Like all the rest, a-lone.

I, of my Spenser quite bereft,
    Last winter sore was shaken ;
Of Lamb I've but a quarter left,
    Nor could I save my Bacon.

My Hall and Hill were levelled flat,
    But Moore was still the cry ;
And then, although I threw them Sprat,
    They swallowed up my Pye.

O'er everything, however slight,
    They seized some airy trammel ;
They snatched my Hogg and Fox one night,
    And pocketed my Campbell.

And then I saw my Crabbe at last,
    Like Hamlet's, backward go ;
And, as my tide was ebbing fast,
    Of course I lost my Rowe.

I wondered into what balloon
　　My books their course had bent ;
And yet, with all my marvelling, soon
　　I found my Marvell went.

My Mallet served to knock me down,
　　Which makes me thus a talker ;
And once, while I was out of town,
　　My Johnson proved a Walker.

While studying o'er the fire one day
　　My Hobbes amidst the smoke,
They bore my Colman clean away,
　　And carried off my Coke.

They picked my Locke, to me far more
　　Than Bramah's patent's worth ;
And now my losses I deplore
　　Without a Home on earth.

If once a book you let them lift,
　　Another they conceal ;
For though I caught them stealing Swift,
　　As swiftly went my Steele.

Hope is not now upon my shelf,
　　Where late he stood elated ;
But, what is strange, my Pope himself
　　Is excommunicated.

My little Suckling in the grave
    Is sunk to swell the ravage;
And what 'twas Crusoe's fate to save
    'Twas mine to lose—a Savage.

Even Glover's works I cannot put
    My frozen hands upon;
Though ever since I lost my Foote
    My Bunyan has been gone.

My Hoyle with Cotton went; oppressed,
    My Taylor too must sail;
To save my Goldsmith from arrest,
    In vain I offered Bayle.

I Prior sought, but could not see
    The Hood so late in front;
And when I turned to hunt for Lee,
    Oh! where was my Leigh Hunt?

I tried to laugh, old Care to tickle,
    Yet could not Tickell touch,
And then, alas! I missed my Mickle,
    And surely mickle's much.

'Tis quite enough my griefs to feed
    My sorrows to excuse,
To think I cannot read my Reid,
    Nor even use my Hughes.

To West, to South, I turn my head,
　　Exposed alike to odd jeers ;
For since my Roger Ascham's fled,
　　I ask 'em for my Rogers.

They took my Horne—and Horne Tooke, too,
　　And thus my treasures flit ;
I feel, when I would Hazlitt view,
　　The flames that it has lit.

My word's worth little, Wordsworth gone,
　　If I survive its doom ;
How many a bard I doated on
　　Was swept off—with my Broome.

My classics would not quiet lie,
　　A thing so fondly hoped ;
Like Dr. Primrose, I may cry,
　　' My Livy has eloped ! '

My life is wasting fast away—
　　I suffer from these shocks ;
And though I've fixed a lock on Gray,
　　There's gray upon my locks.

I'm far from young—am growing pale—
　　I see my Butter fly ;
And when they ask about my *ail*,
　　'Tis Burton ! I reply.

They still have made me slight returns,
　　And thus my griefs divide ;
For oh ! they've cured me of my Burns,
　　And eased my Akenside.

But all I think I shall not say,
　　Nor let my anger burn ;
For as they never found me Gay,
　　They have not left me Sterne.

## BALLADE OF BIBLIOCLASTS.

GRAHAM R. TOMSON. *Longman's Magazine.*

WHERE is that baleful maid
    Who Shakspere's pages shred?
Whose slow diurnal raid
The flames with *Stephen* fed?
Where is *Duke Humphrey* sped?
And where the *Henries'* book?—
They all are vanishèd
With Betty Barnes, the Cook.[1]

And now her ghost dismayed
In woful ways doth tread,—
(Nay, once the weary shade
Sir Walter visited)[2]—
Where culprits sore bestead,
In damp or fiery nook,
Repent their deeds of dread,
With Betty Barnes, the Cook.

[1] Cook of Mr. Warburton, Somerset Herald. She burned, among many other quartos, Shakspere's *Henry I.* and *II.* and *King Stephen.*
[2] See Introduction to *Fortunes of Nigel.*

There Bagford's evil trade
Is fitly punishèd,
And fierce the flames have played
Round Omar's guilty head :
The Biblioclastic Dead
Have diverse pains to brook,
'Mid Rats and Rain-pools led
With Betty Barnes, the Cook.

ENVOY.

Caxton ! be comforted—
For those who wronged thee—look !
They break Affliction's bread
With Betty Barnes, the Cook.

## A TRAITOR.

F. FERTIAULT.          *Les Amoureux du Livre, p.* 28.  *Paris,* 1877.

'TIS here, the Book you begged for so,
    The present that you craved, behold it !
I half distrusted you, you know ;
    And now I've bought it—where you sold it !
I liked you once, the page that told it,
    You've cut, uncut the others though,
    From old esteem you've fallen low,
To vend my book ; you once extolled it !
    'Tis well ; I've learned your lesson, friend,
When next you want a book I've writ,
    I'll add no line of prose nor verse,
    I'll give no book, but take my purse,
    And save you trouble, and extend
A hand that holds the price of it !

                              A. L.

## A DOMESTIC EVENT.

F. FERTIAULT.                    *From ' Les Amoureux du Livre.'*

BACK from a tedious holiday
  He comes, and—Duty first—he looks
 Around for his familiar books;
But all the room's in disarray !
He searches, what's the matter, eh ?
 He hunts in most unheard of nooks.
 'Were robbers here, or were they cooks,
Who seized, who stole my Books away ?
Not one ! What wind has blown about,
What tempest can have tossed them out,
 And cleared the shelves that used to hold them ?'
No cook, no thief, no tempest came,
His lady wife 'tis she's to blame,
 Who carted off the Books—and sold them !

         A. L.

## THE SULTAN OF MY BOOKS.

There is many a true word spoken in doggerel.—*Czech Folk-Song*.

EDMUND GOSSE.

COME hither, my Wither,
    My Suckling, my Dryden !
My Hudibras, hither !
    My Heinsius from Leyden !
Dear Play-books in quarto,
    Fat tomes in brown leather
Stray never too far to
    Come back here together !

I've varied departments
    To give my books shelter ;
Shelves, open apartments
    For tomes helter-skelter ;
These are artisans' flats, fit
    For common editions,—
I find them, as that's fit,
    Good wholesome positions.

But books that I cherish
  Live under glass cases ;
In the waste lest they perish
  I build them oases ;
Where gas cannot find them,
  Where worms cannot grapple,
Those panes hold behind them
  My eye and its apple.


And here you see flirting
  Fine folks of distinction :
Unique books just skirting
  The verge of extinction ;
Old texts with one error
  And long notes upon it ;
The 'Magistrates' Mirror '
  (With Nottingham's sonnet) ;


Tooled Russias to gaze on,
  Moroccos to fondle,
My Denham, in blazon,
  My vellum-backed Vondel,
My Marvell,—a copy
  Was never seen taller,—
My Jones's ' Love's Poppy,'
  My dear little Waller ;

I never upbraid these
    Old periwigged sinners,
Their songs and light ladies,
    Their dances and dinners ;
My book-shelf's a haven
    From storms puritanic,—
Why need they be craven ?
    Of death they've no panic !


My book-room is little,
    And poor are its treasures ;
All pleasures are brittle,
    And so are my pleasures ;
But though I shall never
    Be Beckford or Locker,
While Fate does not sever
    The door from the knocker,


No book shall tap vainly
    At latch or at lattice
(If costumed urbanely,
    And worth our care, that is) ;
In winter or summer,
    My bards in morocco,
Shall shield the new comer
    From storm or sirocco.

.    .    .    .

I might prate thus for pages,
  The theme is so pleasant ;
But the gloom of the ages
  Lies on me at present ;
All business and fear to
  The cold world I banish.
Hush ! like the Ameer, to
  My harem I vanish !

## OUR BOOK-SHELVES.

THOMAS GORDON HAKE.                    *From the ' State' of April 17, 1886.*

WHAT solace would those books afford,
   In gold and vellum cover,
Could men but say them word for word
   Who never turn them over !

Books that must know themselves by heart
   As by endowment vital,
Could they their truths to us impart
   Not stopping with the title !

Line after line their wisdom flows,
   Page after page repeating ;
Yet never on our ears bestows
   A single sound of greeting.

As thus they lie upon the shelves,
   Such wisdom in their pages,
Do they rehearse it to themselves,
   Or rest like silent sages ?

One book we know such fun invokes,
    As well were worth the telling :
Must it not chuckle o'er the jokes
    That it is ever spelling ?

And for the Holy Bible there,
    It greets us with mild teaching ;
Though no one its contents may hear,
    Does it not go on preaching ?

## AMONG MY BOOKS.

FRANCIS ST. CLAIR-ERSKINE,
EARL OF ROSSLYN.
*From ' Sonnets.'* 1883.

ALONE, 'midst living works of mighty dead,
 Poets and Scholars versed in history's lore,
With thoughts that reached beyond them and before,
I dream, and leave their glorious works unread ;
Their greatness numbs me both in heart and head.
I cannot weep with Petrarch, and still more
I fail when I would delve the depths of yore,
And learn old Truths of modern lies instead ;
The shelves frown on me blackly, with a life
That ne'er can die, and helpless to begin,
I can but own my weakness, and deplore
This waste, this barren brain, ah ! once so rife
With hope and fancy. Pardon all my sin,
Great Ghosts that wander on the Eternal Shore.

## THE LIBRARY.

JOHN GODFREY SAXE.

*One of the excerpts from ' Occasional
Poems ' included in his ' Complete
Poems.'*

HERE, e'en the sturdy democrat may find,
　　Nor scorn their rank, the nobles of the mind ;
While kings may learn, nor blush at being shown,
How Learning's patents abrogate their own.
A goodly company and fair to see ;
Royal plebeians ; earls of low degree ;
Beggars whose wealth enriches every clime ;
Princes who scarce can boast a mental dime ;
Crowd here together like the quaint array
Of jostling neighbours on a market day.
Homer and Milton,—can we call them blind ?—
Of godlike sight, the vision of the mind ;
Shakspere, who calmly looked creation through,
' Exhausted worlds, and then imagined new ; '
Plato the sage, so thoughtful and serene,
He seems a prophet by his heavenly mien ;
Shrewd Socrates, whose philosophic power
Xantippe proved in many a trying hour ;

And Aristophanes, whose humour run
In vain endeavour to be-'cloud' the sun ;
Majestic Æschylus, whose glowing page
Holds half the grandeur of the Athenian stage ;
Pindar, whose odes, replete with heavenly fire,
Proclaim the master of the Grecian lyre ;
Anacreon, famed for many a luscious line
Devote to Venus and the god of wine.

I love vast libraries ; yet there is a doubt
If one be better with them or without,—
Unless he use them wisely, and indeed,
Knows the high art of what and how to read.
At learning's fountain it is sweet to drink,
But 'tis a nobler privilege to think ;
And oft from books apart, the thirsting mind
May make the nectar which it cannot find,
'Tis well to borrow from the good and great ;
'Tis wise to learn ; 'tis godlike to create !

## IN THE LIBRARY.

CLINTON SCOLLARD.              *From ' With Reed and Lyre.'* 1886.

FROM the oriels one by one,
 Slowly fades the setting sun ;
On the marge of afternoon
Stands the new-born crescent moon.
In the twilight's crimson glow
Dim the quiet alcoves grow.
Drowsy-lidded Silence smiles
On the long deserted aisles ;
Out of every shadowy nook
Spirit faces seem to look.
Some with smiling eyes, and some
With a sad entreaty dumb ;
He who shepherded his sheep
On the wild Sicilian steep,
He above whose grave are set
Sprays of Roman violet ;
Poets, sages—all who wrought
In the crucible of thought.
Day by day as seasons glide

On the great eternal tide,
Noiselessly they gather thus
In the twilight beauteous,
Hold communion each with each,
Closer than our earthly speech,
Till within the east are born
Premonitions of the morn !

## THE BOOK-HUNTER.

FRANK DEMPSTER SHERMAN.        *From the 'Century Magazine,*
*November,* 1885.

A CUP of coffee, eggs, and rolls
   Sustain him on his morning strolls :
Unconscious of the passers-by,
He trudges on with downcast eye ;
He wears a queer old hat and coat,
Suggestive of a style remote ;
His manner is preoccupied,—
A shambling gait, from side to side.
For him the sleek, bright-windowed shop
Is all in vain,—he does not stop.
His thoughts are fixed on dusty shelves
Where musty volumes hide themselves,—
Rare prints of poetry and prose,
And quaintly lettered folios,—
Perchance a parchment manuscript,
In some forgotten corner slipped,
Or monk-illumined missal bound
In vellum with brass clasps around ;

These are the pictured things that throng
His mind the while he walks along.
A dingy street, a cellar dim,
With book-lined walls, suffices him.
The dust is white upon his sleeves ;
He turns the yellow, dog-eared leaves
With just the same religious look
That priests give to the Holy Book.
He does not heed the stifling air
If so he find a treasure there.
He knows rare books, like precious wines,
Are hidden where the sun ne'er shines ;
For him delicious flavours dwell
In books as in old Muscatel ;
He finds in features of the type
A clew to prove the grape was ripe.
And when he leaves this dismal place,
Behold, a smile lights up his face !
Upon his cheeks a genial glow,—
Within his hand Boccaccio,
A first edition worn with age,
' Firenze' on the title-page.

## BALLADE OF THE BOOK-HUNTER.

A. LANG.                    *From 'Ballades in Blue China.'* 1880.

IN torrid heats of late July,
　　In March, beneath the bitter *bise*,
He book-hunts while the loungers fly,—
He book-hunts, though December freeze ;
In breeches baggy at the knees,
And heedless of the public jeers,
For these, for these, he hoards his fees,—
Aldines, Bodonis, Elzevirs !

No dismal stall escapes his eye,
He turns o'er tomes of low degrees,
There soiled Romanticists may lie,
Or Restoration comedies ;
Each tract that flutters in the breeze
For him is charged with hopes and fears,
In mouldy novels fancy sees
Aldines, Bodonis, Elzevirs !

With restless eyes that peer and spy,
Sad eyes that heed not skies nor trees,

In dismal nooks he loves to pry,
Whose motto evermore is *Spes !*
But ah ! the fabled treasure flees ;
Grown rarer with the fleeting years,
In rich men's shelves they take their ease,
Aldines, Bodonis, Elzevirs !


### ENVOY.

Prince, all the things that tease and please,
Fame, love, wealth, kisses, cheers, and tears,
What are they but such toys as these—
Aldines, Bodonis, Elzevirs ?

## BALLADE OF TRUE WISDOM.

A. LANG. *From ' Ballades in Blue China.'* 1880.

WHILE others are asking for beauty or fame,
  Or praying to know that for which they should
   pray,
Or courting Queen Venus, that affable dame,
Or chasing the Muses, the weary and gray,
The sage has found out a more excellent way,—
To Pan and to Pallas his incense he showers,
And his humble petition puts up day by day,
For a house full of books, and a garden of flowers.

Inventors may bow to the God that is lame,
And crave from the light of his stithy a ray ;
Philosophers kneel to the God without name,
Like the people of Athens, agnostics are they ;
The hunter a fawn to Diana will slay,
The maiden wild roses will wreathe for the Hours,—
But the wise man will ask, ere libation he pay,
For a house full of books, and a garden of flowers.

Oh grant me a life without pleasure or blame
(As mortals count pleasure who rush through their day
With a speed to which that of the tempest is tame),
Oh grant me a house by the beach of a bay,
Where the waves can be surly in winter, and play
With the sea-weed in summer, ye bountiful powers !
And I'd leave all the hurry, the noise, and the fray,
For a house full of books, and a garden of flowers.

### ENVOY.

Gods, give or withhold it ! Your ' yea ' and your ' nay '
Are immutable, heedless of outcry of ours ;
But life *is* worth living,[1] and here we would stay
For a house full of books, and a garden of flowers.

[1] Written seven years ago.—A. L.

## BALLADE OF THE BOOKMAN'S PARADISE.

A. LANG.                                    *From ' Rhymes à la Mode.'* 1885.

THERE *is* a Heaven, or here, or there,—
    A Heaven there is, for me and you,
Where bargains meet for purses spare,
Like ours, are not so far and few.
Thuanus' bees go humming through
The learned groves, 'neath rainless skies,
O'er volumes old and volumes new,
Within that Bookman's Paradise !

There treasures bound for Longepierre
Keep brilliant their morocco blue,
There Hookes' ' Amanda ' is not rare,
Nor early tracts upon Peru !
Racine is common as Rotrou,
No Shakspere Quarto search defies,
And Caxtons grow as blossoms grew,
Within that Bookman's Paradise !

There's Eve,—not our first mother fair,—
But Clovis Eve, a binder true ;
Thither does Bauzonnet repair,
Derome, Le Gascon, Padeloup !
But never come the cropping crew,
That dock a volume's honest size,
Nor they that ' letter ' backs askew,
Within that Bookman's Paradise !

### ENVOY.

Friend, do not Heber and De Thou,
And Scott, and Southey, kind and wise,
*La chasse au bouquin* still pursue
Within that Bookman's Paradise?

## MY SHAKSPERE.

H. C. BUNNER.
*Written expressly for this collection.*

WITH bevelled binding, with uncut edge,
    With broad white margin and gilded top,
Fit for my library's choicest ledge,
    Fresh from the bindery, smelling of shop,
In tinted cloth, with a strange design—
    Buskin and scroll-work and mask and crown,
    And an arabesque legend tumbling down—
'The Works of Shakspere' were never so fine.
Fresh from the shop ! I turn the page—
    Its 'ample margin' is wide and fair—
    Its type is chosen with daintiest care ;
    There's a 'New French Elzevir' strutting there
That would shame its prototypic age.
Fresh from the shop !  O Shakspere mine,
I've half a notion you're much too fine !

There's an ancient volume that I recall,
    In foxy leather much chafed and worn ;
Its back is broken by many a fall,
    The stitchers are loose and the leaves are torn ;

And gone is the bastard-title, next
　　To the title-page scribbled with owners' names,
　　That in straggling old-style type proclaims
That the work is from the corrected text
　　Left by the late Geo. Steevens, Esquire.


　　The broad sky burns like a great blue fire,
And the Lake shines blue as shimmering steel,
　　And it cuts the horizon like a blade—
　　But behind the poplar's a strip of shade—
　　　　The great tall Lombardy on the lawn.
And lying there in the grass, I feel
　　The wind that blows from the Canada shore,
　　And in cool, sweet puffs comes stealing o'er,
　　　　Fresh as any October dawn.


I lie on my breast in the grass, my feet
　　Lifted boy-fashion, and swinging free,
　　The old brown Shakspere in front of me.
And big are my eyes, and my heart's a-beat ;
And my whole soul's lost—in what ?—who knows ?
Perdita's charms or Perdita's woes—
Perdita fairy-like, fair and sweet.
　　Is any one jealous, I wonder, now,
　　Of my love for Perdita ?　For I vow
　　I loved her well.　And who can say
　　That life would be quite the same life to-day—

That Love would mean so much, if she
Had not taught me its A B C ?

The Grandmother, thin and bent and old,
    But her hair still dark and her eyes still bright,
        Totters around among her flowers—
    Old-fashioned flowers of pink and white ;
And turns with a trowel the dark rich mould
    That feeds the blooms of her heart's delight.
        Ah me ! for her and for me the hours
Go by, and for her the smell of earth—
And for me the breeze and a far love's birth,
    And the sun and the sky and all the things
    That a boy's heart hopes and a poet sings.

Fresh from the shop !   O Shakspere mine,
It wasn't the binding made you divine !
    I knew you first in a foxy brown,
    In the old, old home, where I laid me down,
        In the idle summer afternoons,
With you alone in the odorous grass,
        And set your thoughts to the wind's low tunes,
And saw your children rise up and pass—
    And dreamed and dreamed of the things to be,
    Known only, I think, to you and me.

I've hardly a heart for you dressed so fine—
Fresh from the shop, O Shakspere mine !

# OLD BOOKS ARE BEST.

### TO J. H. P.

BEVERLY CHEW.                    *From the ' Critic' of March* 13, 1886.

O LD Books are best !   With what delight
    Does ' Faithorne fecit ' greet our sight
On frontispiece or title-page
Of that old time, when on the stage
' Sweet Nell ' set ' Rowley's ' heart alight !

And you, O Friend, to whom I write,
Must not deny, e'en though you might,
    Through fear of modern pirate's rage,
       Old Books are best.

What though the prints be not so bright,
The paper dark, the binding slight?
    Our author, be he dull or sage,
    Returning from that distant age
So lives again, we say of right :
       Old Books are best.

## THE FORGOTTEN BOOKS.

THOMAS S. COLLIER.                    *Written expressly for this collection.*

HID by the garret's dust, and lost
　　Amid the cobwebs wreathed above,
They lie, these volumes that have cost
　　Such weeks of hope and waste of love.

The Theologian's garnered lore
　　Of Scripture text, and words divine ;
And verse, that to some fair one bore
　　Thoughts that like fadeless stars would shine ;

The grand wrought epics, that were born
　　From mighty throes of heart and brain,—
Here rest, their covers all unworn,
　　And all their pages free from stain.

Here lie the chronicles that told
　　Of man, and his heroic deeds—
Alas ! the words once 'writ in gold '
　　Are tarnished so that no one reads.

And tracts that smote each other hard,
   While loud the friendly plaudits rang,
All animosities discard,
   Where old, moth-eaten garments hang.

The heroes that were made to strut
   In tinsel on 'life's mimic stage'
Found, all too soon, the deepening rut
   Which kept them silent in the page;

And heroines, whose loveless plight
   Should wake the sympathetic tear,
In volumes sombre as the night
   Sleep on through each succeeding year.

Here Phyllis languishes forlorn,
   And Strephon waits beside his flocks,
And early huntsmen wind the horn,
   Within the boundaries of a box.

Here, by the irony of fate,
   Beside the 'peasant's humble board,'
The monarch 'flaunts his robes of state,'
   And spendthrifts find the miser's hoard.

Days come and go, and still we write,
   And hope for some far happier lot
Than that our work should meet this blight—
   And yet—some books must be forgot.

## PICTURE-BOOKS IN WINTER.

ROBERT LOUIS STEVENSON.     *From ' A Child's Garden of Verses.'*   1885.

S UMMER fading, winter comes—
    Frosty mornings, tingling thumbs,
Window robins, winter rooks,
And the picture story-books.

Water now is turned to stone
Nurse and I can walk upon ;
Still we find the flowing brooks
And the picture story-books.

All the pretty things put by,
Wait upon the children's eye,
Sheep and shepherds, trees and crooks,
In the picture story-books.

We may see how all things are,
Seas and cities, near and far,
And the flying fairies' looks,
In the picture story-books.

How am I to sing your praise,
Happy chimney-corner days,
Sitting safe in nursery nooks,
Reading picture story-books?

## COMPANIONS.

A French writer (whom I love well) speaks of three kinds of companions :
men, women, and books. SIR JOHN DAVYS.

RICHARD HENRY STODDARD. *From the ' Atlantic Monthly,' June,* 1877.

WE have companions, comrade mine :
 Jolly good fellows, tried and true,
Are filling their cups with the Rhenish wine,
 And pledging each other, as I do you.
Never a man in all the land
 But has, in his hour of need, a friend,
Who stretches to him a helping hand
 And stands by him to the bitter end.
If not before, there is comfort then,
In the strong companionship of men.

But better than that, old friend of mine,
 Is the love of woman, the life of life,
Whether in maiden's eyes it shine,
 Or melts in the tender kiss of wife ;
A heart contented to feel, not know,
 That finds in the other its sole delight ;

White hands that are loth to let us go,
  The tenderness that is more than might !
On earth below, in heaven above,
Is there anything better than woman's love ?

I do not say so, companion mine,
  For what, without it, would I be here ?
It lightens my troubles, like this good wine,
  And, if I must weep, sheds tear for tear !
But books, old friends that are always new,
  Of all good things that we know are best ;
They never forsake us, as others do,
  And never disturb our inward rest.
Here is truth in a world of lies,
And all that in man is great and wise !

Better than men and women, friend,
  That are dust, though dear in our joy and pain,
Are the books their cunning hands have penned,
  For they depart, but the books remain ;
Through these they speak to us what was best
  In the loving heart and the noble mind :
All their royal souls possessed
  Belongs forever to all mankind !
When others fail him, the wise man looks
To the sure companionship of books.

## AMONG MY BOOKS.

SAMUEL MINTURN PECK.                    *From ' Cap and Bells.'* 1886.

A MONG my books—what rest is there
    From wasting woes ! what balm for care !
  If ills appal or clouds hang low,
  And drooping, dim the fleeting show,
I revel still in visions rare.
At will I breathe the classic air,
The wanderings of Ulysses share ;
  Or see the plume of Bayard flow
      Among my books.

Whatever face the world may wear—
If Lillian has no smile to spare,
  For others let her beauty blow,
  Such favours I can well forego ;
Perchance forget the frowning fair
      Among my books.

## THE BOOK BATTALION.

GEORGE PARSONS LATHROP.  *Written for the present collection.*

WHEREVER I go, there's a trusty battalion
 That follows me faithfully, steady, and true ;
Their force, when I falter, I safely may rally on,
 Knowing their stoutness will carry me through:
Some fifteen hundred in order impartial,
 So ranged that they tell what they mean by their looks.
Of all the armies the world can marshal
 There are no better soldiers than well-tried books.


Dumb in their ranks on the shelves imprisoned,
 They never retreat.   Give the word, and they'll fire !
A few with scarlet and gold are bedizened,
 But many muster in rough attire ;
And some, with service and scars grown wizened,
 Seem hardly the mates for their fellows in youth ;
Yet they, and the troops armed only with quiz and
 Light laughter, all battle alike for the truth.

Here are those who gave motive to sock and to buskin ;
  With critics, historians, poets galore ;
A cheaply uniformed set of Ruskin,
  Which Ruskin would hate from his heart's very core ;
Molière ('99), an old calf-bound edition,
  ' *De Pierre Didot l'aîné, et de Firmin Didot,*'
Which, meek and demure, with a sort of contrition,
  Is masking its gun-lights, with fun all aglow ;

And Smollett and Fielding, as veterans battered—
  Cloth stripped from their backs, and their sides out
      of joint,
Their pictures of life all naked and tattered
  Being thus applied to themselves with a point ;
And six or eight books that I wrote myself,
  To look at which, even, I'm half afraid ;
They brought me more labour and pleasure than pelf,
  And are clamouring still because they're not paid.

But these raw levies remain still faithful,
  Because they know that volumes old
Stand by me, although their eyes dim and wraithful
  Remind me they seldom at profit were sold.
So I say, be they splendid or tatterdemalion,
  If only you know what they mean by their looks,
You will never find a better battalion
  Of soldiers to serve you than well-tried books.

## ON THE FLY-LEAF OF A BOOK OF OLD PLAYS.

WALTER LEARNED.          *Written for the present collection.*

AT Cato's-Head in Russell Street
  These leaves she sat a-stitching ;
I fancy she was trim and neat,
  Blue-eyed and quite bewitching.

Before her, in the street below,
  All powder, ruffs, and laces,
There strutted idle London beaux
  To ogle pretty faces ;

While, filling many a Sedan chair
  With hoop and monstrous feather,
In patch and powder London's fair
  Went trooping past together.

Swift, Addison, and Pope, mayhap
  They sauntered slowly past her,
Or printer's boy, with gown and cap
  For Steele, went trotting faster.

For beau nor wit had she a look,
   Nor lord nor lady minding ;
She bent her head above this book,
   Attentive to her binding.

And one stray thread of golden hair,
   Caught on her nimble fingers,
Was stitched within this volume, where
   Until to-day it lingers.

Past and forgotten, beaux and fair ;
   Wigs, powder, all out-dated ;
A queer antique, the Sedan chair ;
   Pope, stiff and antiquated.

Yet as I turn these odd old plays,
   This single stray lock finding,
I'm back in those forgotten days
   And watch her at her binding.

## FROM THE FLY-LEAF OF THE ROWFANT MONTAIGNE (FLORIO, 1603).

FREDERICK LOCKER.

OF yore, when books were few and fine,
Will Shakspere cut these leaves of mine,
But when he passed I went astray
Till bought by Pope, a gift for Gay.
Then, later on, betwixt my pages
A nose was poked—the Bolt-Court Sage's.

But though the Fame began with Rawleigh,
And had not dwindled with Macaulay,
Though still I tincture many tomes
Like Lowell's pointed sense, and Holmes',
For me the halcyon days have past—
I'm here, and with a dunce at last.

## MY BOOKS.

HENRY WADSWORTH LONGFELLOW. *Written in December*, 1881.

SADLY as some old mediæval knight
   Gazed at the arms he could no longer wield,
  The sword two-handed and the shining shield
  Suspended in the hall, and full in sight,
While secret longings for the lost delight
  Of tourney or adventure in the field
  Came over him, and tears but half concealed
  Trembled and fell upon his beard of white,
So I behold these books upon their shelf,
  My ornaments and arms of other days ;
  Not wholly useless, though no longer used,
For they remind me of my other self,
  Younger and stronger, and the pleasant ways,
  In which I walked, now clouded and confused.

## DE LIBRIS.

COSMO MONKHOUSE. *Written for the present collection.*

TRUE—there are books and books.    There's
　　Gray,
　　For instance, and there's Bacon ;
There's Longfellow, and Monstrelet,
　　And also Colton's ' Lacon,'
With ' Laws of Whist ' and those of Libel,
And Euclid, and the Mormon Bible.

And some are dear as friends, and some
　　We keep because we need them ;
And some we ward from worm and thumb,
　　And love too well to read them.
My own are poor, and mostly new,
But I've an Elzevir or two.

That as a gift is prized, the next
　　For trouble in the finding ;
This Aldine for its early text,
　　That Plantin for the binding ;
This sorry Herrick hides a flower,
The record of one perfect hour.

But whether it be worth or looks
    We gently love or strongly,
Such virtue doth reside in books
    We scarce can love them wrongly ;
To sages an eternal school,
A hobby (harmless) to the fool.

Nor altogether fool is he
    Who orders, free from doubt,
Those books which ' no good library
    Should ever be without,'
And blandly locks the well-glazed door
On tomes that issue never more.

Less may we scorn his cases grand,
    Where safely, surely linger
Fair virgin fields of type, unscanned
    And innocent of finger.
There rest, preserved from dust accurst,
The first editions — and the worst.

And least of all should we that write
    With easy jest deride them,
Who hope to leave when ' lost to sight '
    The best of us inside them,
Dear shrines ! where many a scribbler's name
Has lasted—longer than his fame.

## EX LIBRIS.

ARTHUR J. MUNBY.

M AN that is born of woman finds a charm
    In that which he is born of.  She it is
Who moulds him with a frown or with a kiss
To good or ill, to welfare or to harm :
But, when he has attain'd her soft round arm
    And drawn it through his own, and made her his,
    He through her eyes beholds a wider bliss,
As sweet as that she gives him, and as warm.

What bliss ?  We dare not name it : her fond looks
    Are jealous too ; she hardly understands,
        Girt by her children's laughter or their cries,
The stately smooth companionship of books :
    And yet to her we owe it, to her hands
        And to her heart, that books can make us wise.

## ON AN INSCRIPTION.

ARTHUR J. MUNBY.

*'Edward Danenhill : Book given him by*
*Joseph Wise, April ye 27th, 1741,' was*
*the inscription in a copy of Carew's*
*'Poems:' (1651.)*

A MAN unknown this volume gave,
    So long since, to his unknown friend,
Ages ago, their lives had end,
And each in some obscurest grave
Lies mixt with earth : none now would care
To ask or who or what they were.

    But, though these two are underground,
Their book is here, all safe and sound ;
And he who wrote it (yea, and more
Than a whole hundred years before)
He, the trim courtier, old Carew,
And all the loves he feign'd or knew,
Have won from Aphrodite's eye
Some show of immortality.

    'Tis ever thus ; by Nature's will
The gift outlasts the giver still ;
And Love itself lives not so long
As doth a lover's feeblest song.

But doubly hard is that man's case,
For whom and for his earnest rhymes
Neither his own nor after-times
Have any work, have any place :
Who through a hundred years shall find
No echoing voice, no answering mind ;
And, when this tann'd and tawny page
Has one more century of age,
And others buy the book anew,
Because they care for old Carew,
Not one who reads shall care or know
What name was his, who owns it now :
But all he wrote and all he did
Shall be in such oblivion hid
As hides the blurr'd and broken stones
That cover his forgotten bones.

## THE LIBRARY.

JOHN GREENLEAF WHITTIER.        *Sung at the opening of the library at*
                                    *Haverhill, Mass.*

'LET there be Light !' God spake of old,
      And over chaos dark and cold,
And through the dead and formless frame
Of nature, life and order came.

Faint was the light at first that shone
On giant fern and mastodon,
On half-formed plant and beast of prey,
And man as rude and wild as they.

Age after age, like waves o'erran
The earth, uplifting brute and man ;
And mind, at length, in symbols dark
Its meanings traced on stone and bark.

On leaf of palm, on sedge-wrought roll,
On plastic clay and leathern scroll,
Man wrote his thoughts ; the ages passed,
And lo ! the Press was found at last !

Then dead souls woke ; the thoughts of men
Whose bones were dust revived again ;
The cloister's silence found a tongue,
Old prophets spake, old poets sung.

And here, to-day, the dead look down,
The kings of mind again we crown ;
We hear the voices lost so long,
The sage's word, the sibyl's song.

Here Greek and Roman find themselves
Alive along these crowded shelves ;
And Shakspere treads again his stage,
And Chaucer paints anew his age.

As if some Pantheon's marbles broke
Their stony trance, and lived and spoke,
Life thrills along the alcoved hall,
The lords of thought await our call.

## LITERATURE AND NATURE.

SAMUEL WADDINGTON.                 *Written for the present collection.*

'MID Cambrian heights around Dolgelly vale,
　　What time we scaled great Cader's rugged pile,
　Or loitered idly where still meadows smile
Beside the Mawddach-stream, or far Cynfael—
Nor tome, nor rhythmic page, nor pastoral tale,
　Our summer-sated senses would beguile ;
　Or lull our ears to melody, the while
The voiceful rill ran lilting down the dale.
In London town once more—behold, once more
　The old delight returns !　'Mid heights how vast,
　In Milton's verse, through what dim paths we wind ;
How Keats's canvas glows, and Wordsworth's lore,
　As tarn or torrent pure, by none surpass'd,
　Sheds light and love—unfathomed, undefined.

## OLD BOOKS, FRESH FLOWERS.

JOSEPH BOULMIER.                    *Rimes Loyales, Paris.* 1857.

A LONE, at home, I dwell, content and free,
    The soft May sun comes with his greeting fair ;
And, like a lute, my heart thrills tremblingly
By the Spring's fingers touched to some sweet air.
Blessed be thou my God, who from my face
Tak'st the pale cast of thought that weary lowers !
My chamber walls—my narrow window-space
Hold all most dear to me : old books, fresh flowers.

Those trusty friends, that faithful company—
My books—say, 'Long his slumbers, and we wait !'
But my flowers murmur as they look on me,
'Nay, never chide him, for he watched so late !'
Brethren and sisters, these of mine ! my room
Shines fair as with the light of Eden's bowers ;
The Louvre is not worth my walls abloom
With all most dear to me : old books, fresh flowers.

Beside your shelves I know not weariness
My silent-speaking books ! so kind and wise ;
And fairer seems your yellowed parchment dress
Than gay morocco, to my loving eyes.
Dear blossoms ! of the humble hermit's choice,
In sweetest communing what joys are ours !
To you I listen, and with you rejoice,
For all I love is here : old books, fresh flowers.


Men are unlovely, but their works are fair,
Aye, men are evil, but their books are good,
The clay hath perished and the soul laid bare
Shines from their books in heavenly solitude.
Light on each slender stem pure blossoms rest,
Like angel envoys of the Heavenly powers ;
Of all earth's maidens these are first and best,
And all I love is here : old books, fresh flowers.


A double harvest crowns my granary :
From all light loves and joys my soul takes flight ;
My books are blossoms and their bee am I,
And God's own volumes are my blossoms bright.
These and no other bosom-friends are mine,
With them, I pass my best, my calmest hours,
These only lead me to the light Divine,
And all I love is here : old books, fresh flowers.

My books are tombs where wit and wisdom sleep,
Stored full with treasure of the long ago ;
My tender buds that dews of springtide steep
Like shining mirrors of the future show.
The present is so sad ! . . . . this dark to-day
Like skies with thunder charged, above us lowers :
Ah ! of the past—the future—speak alway,
Tell me of naught but these . . . . old books, fresh
    flowers.

GRAHAM R. TOMSON.

## THE COUNTRY SQUIRE.

TOMAS YRIARTE.                    *An anonymous translation of one of the
                                        'Literary Fables.'*

A COUNTRY squire, of greater wealth than wit
   (For fools are often blessed with fortune's smile),
Had built a splendid house, and furnished it
            In splendid style.

' One thing is wanting,' said a friend ; ' for, though
   The rooms are fine, the furniture profuse,
You lack a library, dear sir, for show,
            If not for use.'

' 'Tis true ; but 'zounds ! ' replied the squire with glee,
   ' The lumber-room in yonder northern wing
(I wonder I ne'er thought of it) will be
           The very thing.

' I'll have it fitted up without delay
   With shelves and presses of the newest mode
And rarest wood, befitting every way
           A squire's abode.

' And when the whole is ready, I'll despatch
　　My coachman—a most knowing fellow—down
To buy me, by admeasurement, a batch
　　　　　　Of books in town.'

But ere the library was half supplied
　　With all its pomps of cabinet and shelf,
The booby squire repented him, and cried
　　　　　　Unto himself :—

' This room is much more roomy than I thought ;
　　Ten thousand volumes hardly would suffice
To fill it, and would cost, however bought,
　　　　　　A plaguy price.

' Now, as I only want them for their looks,
　　It might, on second thoughts, be just as good,
And cost me next to nothing, if the books,
　　　　　　Were made of wood.

' It shall be so, I'll give the shaven deal
　　A coat of paint—a colourable dress,
To look like calf or vellum, and conceal
　　　　　　Its nakedness.

' And, gilt and lettered with the author's name,
　　Whatever is most excellent and rare
Shall be, or seem to be ('tis all the same),
　　　　　　Assembled there.'

The work was done ; the simulated hoards
   Of wit and wisdom round the chamber stood,
In binding some ; and some, of course, in *boards*,
         Where all were wood.

From bulky folios down to slender twelves
   The choicest tomes, in many an even row
Displayed their lettered backs upon the shelves,
         A goodly show.

With such a stock as seemingly surpassed
   The best collection ever formed in Spain,
What wonder if the owner grew at last
         Supremely vain ?

What wonder, as he paced from shelf to shelf,
   And conned their titles, that the squire began,
Despite his ignorance, to think himself
         A learned man ?

*Let every amateur, who merely looks*
   *To backs and binding, take the hint, and sell*
*His costly library—for painted books*
         *Would serve as well.*

## LOVE AND BOOKS.

EDMUND GOSSE. *From the Swedish of K. D. af Wirsén.*

STILL dumb thou sittest, with a downcast look,
The world forgetting o'er a brown old book ;

While she who would be always near thee tries
In silence to embrace thee with her eyes.

Say not so sharply ' Leave me here in peace ! '
Nay ! leave thy book, and from dull reading cease ;

Since many a man who sits alone, perplexed,
Would yield all else to be so teased and vexed.

Give up thy book of life for Love to paint
With golden pictures of a household saint,

With miniatures whose blazon may provide
For days that shall grow dark a light and guide ;

So when thou turn'st the page where love struck blind
Thy bookish eyes, an angel thou shalt find.

# APPENDIX.

# THE BIBLIOMANIA.

Hic, inquis, veto quisquam faxit oletum.
Pinge duos angues.
Pers. Sat. i. l. 112.

JOHN FERRIAR. An Epistle to Richard Heber, Esq.<br>Manchester, April, 1809.

WHAT wild desires, what restless torments seize
   The hapless man, who feels the book-disease,
If niggard Fortune cramp his gen'rous mind
And Prudence quench the Spark by heaven assign'd!
With wistful glance his aching eyes behold
The Princeps-copy, clad in blue and gold,
Where the tall Book-case, with partition thin,
Displays, yet guards the tempting charms within :
So great Facardin view'd, as sages [1] tell,
Fair Crystalline immur'd in lucid cell.

Not thus the few, by happier fortune grac'd,
And blest, like you, with talents, wealth, and taste,
Who gather nobly, with judicious hand,
The Muse's treasures from each letter'd strand.

---

[1] *Sages,* Count Hamilton, in the *Quatre Facardins,* and Mr. M. Lewis, in his *Tales of Romance.*

For you the Monk illum'd his pictur'd page,
For you the press defies the Spoils of age ;
FAUSTUS for you infernal tortures bore,
For you ERASMUS [1] starv'd on Adria's shore.
The FOLIO-ALDUS loads your happy Shelves,
And dapper ELZEVIRS, like fairy elves,
Shew their light forms amidst the well-gilt Twelves :
In slender type the GIOLITOS shine,
And bold BODONI stamps his Roman line.
For you the LOUVRE opes its regal doors,
And either DIDOT lends his brilliant stores :
With faultless types, and costly sculptures bright,
IBARRA'S Quixote charms your ravish'd sight :
LABORDE in splendid tablets shall explain
Thy beauties, glorious, tho' unhappy SPAIN !
O hallowed name, the theme of future years,
Embalm'd in Patriot-blood, and England's tears,
Be thine fresh honours from the tuneful tongue,
By Isis' stream which mourning Zion sung !

But devious oft from ev'ry classic Muse,
The keen Collector meaner paths will choose :
And first the Margin's breadth his soul employs,
Pure, snowy, broad, the type of nobler joys.

---

[1] See the 'Opulentia Sordida,' in his *Colloquies*, where he complains
feelingly of the spare Venetian diet.

In vain might HOMER roll the tide of song,
Or HORACE smile, or TULLY charm the throng;
If crost by Pallas' ire, the trenchant blade
Or too oblique, or near, the edge invade,
The Bibliomane exclaims, with haggard eye,
' No Margin !' turns in haste, and scorns to buy.
He turns where PYBUS rears his Atlas-head,
Or MADOC'S mass conceals its veins of lead.
The glossy lines in polish'd order stand,
While the vast margin spreads on either hand,
Like Russian wastes, that edge the frozen deep,
Chill with pale glare, and lull to mortal sleep.[1]

Or English books, neglected and forgot,
Excite his wish in many a dusty lot :
Whatever trash *Midwinter* gave to-day,
Or *Harper's* rhiming sons, in paper gray,
At ev'ry auction, bent on fresh supplies,
He cons his Catalogue with anxious eyes :
Where'er the slim Italics mark the page,
*Curious and rare* his ardent mind engage.
Unlike the Swans, in Tuscan Song display'd,
He hovers eager o'er Oblivion's Shade,

---

[1] It may be said that Quintilian recommends margins; but it is with a view to their being occasionally occupied : 'Debet vacare etiam locus, in quo notentur quæ scribentibus solent extra ordinem, id est ex aliis quam qui sunt in manibus loci, occurrere. Irrumpunt enim optimi nonnunquam Sensus, quos neque inserere oportet, neque differre tutum est.' *Instit.* lib. x. c. 3.
He was therefore no *Margin-man*, in the modern sense.

To snatch obscurest names from endless night,
And give COKAIN or FLETCHER [1] back to light.
In red morocco drest he loves to boast
The bloody murder, or the yelling ghost ;
Or dismal ballads, sung to crouds of old,
Now cheaply bought for thrice their weight in gold.
Yet to th' unhonour'd dead be Satire just ;
Some flow'rs [2] 'smell sweet and blossom in their dust.'
'Tis thus ev'n SHIRLEY boasts a golden line,
And LOVELACE strikes, by fits, a note divine.
Th' unequal gleams like midnight-lightnings play,
And deepen'd gloom succeeds, in place of day.

But human bliss still meets some envious storm ;
He droops to view his PAYNTERS' mangled form :
Presumptuous grief, while pensive Taste repines
O'er the frail relics of her Attic Shrines !
O for that power, for which Magicians vye,
To look through earth, and secret hoards descry !
I'd spurn such gems as Marinel [3] beheld,

---

[1] Fletcher, a translator of Martial.   A very bad poet, but *exceedingly
scarce.*

[2] Only the actions of the just
Smell sweet, and blossom in the dust.
                                        SHIRLEY.
Perhaps Shirley had in view this passage of Persius,—

Nunc non e tumulo fortunataque favilla
Nascentur Violæ?
                                        *Sat.* i. l. 37.

[3] *Faërie Queene.*

And all the wealth Aladdin's cavern held,
Might I divine in what mysterious gloom
The rolls of sacred bards have found their tomb :
Beneath what mould'ring tower, or waste champain,
Is hid MENANDER, sweetest of the train :
Where rests ANTIMACHUS' forgotten lyre,
Where gentle SAPPHO's still seductive fire ;
Or he,[1] whom chief the laughing Muses own,
Yet skill'd with softest accents to bemoan
Sweet Philomel [2] in strains so like her own.

The menial train has prov'd the Scourge of wit,
Ev'n OMAR burnt less Science than the spit.
Earthquakes and wars remit their deadly rage,
But ev'ry feast demands some fated page.
Ye Towers of Julius,[3] ye alone remain
Of all the piles that saw our nation's stain,
When HARRY's sway opprest the groaning realm,
And Lust and Rapine seiz'd the wav'ring helm.
Then ruffian-hands defaced the sacred fanes,
Their saintly statues and their storied panes ;
Then from the chest, with ancient art embost,
The Penman's pious scrolls were rudely tost ;
Then richest manuscripts, profusely spread,
The brawny Churls' devouring Oven fed :

---

[1] Aristophanes.
[2] See his exquisite hymn to the Nightingale in his Ὄρνιθες.
[3] Gray.

And thence Collectors date the heav'nly ire
That wrapt Augusta's domes in sheets of fire.[1]

Taste, tho' misled, may yet some purpose gain,
But Fashion guides a book-compelling train.[2]
Once, far apart from Learning's moping crew,
The travell'd beau display'd his red heel'd shoe,
Till ORFORD rose, and told of rhiming Peers,
Repeating *noble* words to polish'd ears ;[3]
Taught the gay croud to prize a flutt'ring name,
In trifling toil'd, nor ' blush'd to find it fame.'
The letter'd fop, now takes a larger scope,
With classic furniture, design'd by HOPE,
(HOPE whom Upholst'rers eye with mute despair,
The doughty pedant of an elbow-chair ;)
Now warm'd by ORFORD, and by GRANGER
      school'd
In Paper-books, superbly gilt and tool'd,
He pastes, from injur'd volumes snipt away,
His *English Heads*, in chronicled array.
Torn from their destin'd page (unworthy meed
Of knightly counsel, and heroic deed)
Not FAITHORNE'S stroke, nor FIELD'S own types
      can save

---

[1] The fire of London.
[2] Cloud-compelling Jove.—Pope's *Iliad*.
[3] . . . gaudent prænomine molles
Auriculæ.

[1]The gallant Veres, and one-eyed OGLE brave.
Indignant readers seek the image fled,
And curse the busy fool, who *wants a head*.

Proudly he shews, with many a smile elate
The scrambling subjects of the *private plate* ;
While Time their actions and their names bereaves,
They grin for ever in the guarded leaves.

Like Poets, born, in vain Collectors strive
To cross their Fate, and learn the art to thrive.
Like Cacus, bent to tame their struggling will,
The Tyrant-passion drags them backward still :
Ev'n I, debarr'd of ease, and studious hours,
Confess, mid' anxious toil, its lurking pow'rs.
How pure the joy, when first my hands unfold
The small, rare volume, black with tarnish'd gold !
The Eye skims restless, like the roving bee,
O'er flowers of wit, or song, or repartee,
While sweet as Springs, new-bubbling from the stone,
Glides through the breast some pleasing theme un-
 known.
Now dipt in ROSSI'S [2] terse and classic style,
His harmless tales awake a transient smile.

[1] *The gallant Veres and one-eyed Ogle.* Three fine heads, for the sake of which the beautiful and interesting ' Commentaries' of Sir Francis Vere have been mutilated by the Collectors of English portraits.

[2] Generally known by the name of James Nicius Erythræus. The allusion is to his *Pinacotheca.*

Now BOUCHET'S motley stores my thoughts arrest,
With wond'rous reading, and with learned jest.
Bouchet [1] whose tomes a grateful line demand,
The valued gift of STANLEY'S lib'ral hand.
Now sadly pleased, through faded Rome I stray,
And mix regrets with gentle DU BELLAY ; [2]
Or turn, with keen delight, the curious page,
Where hardly Pasquin [3] braves the Pontiff's rage.

But D——n's strains should tell the sad reverse,
When Business calls, invet'rate foe to verse !
Tell how ' the Demon claps his iron hands,'
' Waves his lank locks, and scours along the lands.'
Through wintry blasts, or summer's fire I go,
To scenes of danger, and to sights of woe.
Ev'n when to Margate ev'ry Cockney roves,
And brainsick-poets long for shelt'ring groves,
Whose lofty shades exclude the noontide glow,
While Zephyrs breathe, and waters trill below, [4]
Me rigid Fate averts, by tasks like these,
From heav'nly musings, and from letter'd ease.

---

[1] *Les Serées de Guillaume Bouchet,* a book of uncommon rarity.  I possess
a handsome copy by the kindness of Colonel Stanley.

[2] *Les Regrets,* by Joachim du Bellay, contains a most amusing and instruc-
tive account of Rome in the sixteenth century.

[3] *Pasquillorum Tomi duo.*

[4] Errare per lucos, amœnæ
     Quos et aquæ subeunt et auræ.
                              HORAT.

Such wholesome checks the better Genius sends,
From dire rehearsals to protect our friends :
Else when the social rites our joys renew,
The stuff 'd Portfolio would alarm your view,
Whence volleying rhimes your patience would o'ercome,
And, spite of kindness, drive you early home.
So when the traveller's hasty footsteps glide
Near smoking lava on Vesuvio's side,
Hoarse-mutt'ring thunders from the depths proceed,
And spouting fires incite his eager speed.
Appall'd he flies, while rattling show'rs invade,
Invoking ev'ry Saint for instant aid :
Breathless, amaz'd, he seeks the distant shore,
And vows to tempt the dang'rous gulph no more.

## THE LIBRARY.

GEORGE CRABBE.      *In want and danger, the unknown poet sent this poem to Edmund Burke, who saw its merit, befriended its author, and procured its publication.*

WHEN the sad soul, by care and grief oppressed,
    Looks round the world, but looks in vain
      for rest,
When every object that appears in view
Partakes her gloom and seems dejected too ;
Where shall affliction from itself retire ?
Where fade away and placidly expire ?
Alas ! we fly to silent scenes in vain ;
Care blasts the honours of the flowery plain ;
Care veils in clouds the sun's meridian beam,
Sighs through the grove, and murmurs in the stream ;
For when the soul is labouring in despair,
In vain the body breathes a purer air :
No storm-tost sailor sighs for slumbering seas—
He dreads the tempest, but invokes the breeze ;
On the smooth mirror of the deep resides
Reflected woe, and o'er unruffled tides
The ghost of every former danger glides.

Thus, in the calms of life, we only see
A steadier image of our misery ;
But lively gales and gently clouded skies
Disperse the sad reflections as they rise ;
And busy thoughts and little cares avail
To ease the mind, when rest and reason fail.
When the dull thought, by no designs employed,
Dwells on the past, or suffered or enjoyed,
We bleed anew in every former grief,
And joys departed furnish no relief.

   Not Hope herself, with all her flattering art,
Can cure this stubborn sickness of the heart :
The soul disdains each comfort she prepares,
And anxious searches for congenial cares ;
Those lenient cares, which, with our own combined,
By mixed sensations ease th' afflicted mind,
And steal our grief away, and leave their own behind ;
A lighter grief ! which feeling hearts endure
Without regret, nor e'en demand a cure.

   But what strange art, what magic can dispose
The troubled mind to change its native woes ?
Or lead us, willing from ourselves, to see
Others more wretched, more undone than we ?
This Books can do ;—nor this alone ; they give
New views of life, and teach us how to live ;
They soothe the grieved, the stubborn they chastise,
Fools they admonish and confirm the wise :

Their aid they yield to all : they never shun
The man of sorrow, nor the wretch undone :
Unlike the hard, the selfish, and the proud,
They fly not sullen from the suppliant crowd ;
Nor tell to various people various things,
But show to subjects what they show to kings.
Come, Child of Care ! to make thy soul serene,
Approach the treasures of this tranquil scene ;
Survey the dome, and, as the doors unfold,
The soul's best cure, in all her cares behold !
Where mental wealth the poor in thought may find,
And mental physic the diseased in mind ;
See here the balms that passion's wounds assuage ;
See coolers here, that damp the fire of rage ;
Here alteratives, by slow degrees control
The chronic habits of the sickly soul ;
And round the heart, and o'er the aching head,
Mild opiates here their sober influence shed.
Now bid thy soul man's busy scenes exclude,
And view composed this silent multitude :—
Silent they are—but though deprived of sound,
Here all the living languages abound ;
Here all that live no more ; preserved they lie,
In tombs that open to the curious eye.

   Blest be the gracious Power, who taught mankind
To stamp a lasting image of the mind !
Beasts may convey, and tuneful birds may sing,

Their mutual feelings, in the opening spring ;
But Man alone has skill and power to send
The heart's warm dictates to the distant friend ;
'Tis his alone to please, instruct, advise
Ages remote, and nations yet to rise.

   In sweet repose, when Labour's children sleep,
When Joy forgets to smile and Care to weep,
When Passion slumbers in the lover's breast,
And Fear and Guilt partake the balm of rest,
Why then denies the studious man to share
Man's common good, who feels his common care ?

   Because the hope is his that bids him fly
Night's soft repose, and sleep's mild power defy,
That after-ages may repeat his praise,
And fame's fair meed be his, for length of days.
Delightful prospect ! when we leave behind
A worthy offspring of the fruitful mind !
Which, born and nursed through many an anxious day,
Shall all our labour, all our care repay.

   Yet all are not these births of noble kind,
Not all the children of a vigorous mind ;
But where the wisest should alone preside,
The weak would rule us, and the blind would guide ;
Nay, man's best efforts taste of man, and show
The poor and troubled source from which they flow ;
Where most he triumphs we his wants perceive,
And for his weakness in his wisdom grieve.

But though imperfect all ; yet wisdom loves
This seat serene, and virtue's self approves :—
Here come the grieved, a change of thought to find ;
The curious here to feed a craving mind ;
Here the devout their peaceful temple choose ;
And here the poet meets his favouring Muse.

With awe, around these silent walks I tread ;
These are the lasting mansions of the dead :—
' The dead !' methinks a thousand tongues reply ;
' These are the tombs of such as cannot die !
Crowned with eternal fame, they sit sublime,
And laugh at all the little strife of time.

Hail, then, immortals ! ye who shine above,
Each, in his sphere, the literary Jove ;
And ye, the common people of these skies,
A humbler crowd of nameless deities ;
Whether 'tis yours to lead the willing mind
Through History's mazes, and the turnings find ;
Or, whether led by Science, ye retire,
Lost and bewildered in the vast desire ;
Whether the Muse invites you to her bowers,
And crowns your placid brows with living flowers !
Or godlike Wisdom teaches you to show
The noblest road to happiness below ;
Or men and manners prompt the easy page
To mark the flying follies of the age ;
Whatever good ye boast, that good impart ;

Inform the head and rectify the heart.

   Lo, all in silence, all in order stand,
And mighty folios first, a lordly band ;
Then quartos their well-ordered ranks maintain,
And light octavos fill a spacious plain :
See yonder, ranged in more frequented rows,
A humbler band of duodecimos ;
While undistinguish'd trifles swell the scene,
The last new play and frittered magazine.
Thus 'tis in life, where first the proud, the great,
In leagued assembly keep their cumbrous state :
Heavy and huge, they fill the world with dread,
Are much admired, and are but little read :
The commons next, a middle rank, are found ;
Professions fruitful pour their offspring round ;
Reasoners and wits are next their place allowed,
And last, of vulgar tribes a countless crowd.

   First, let us view the form, the size, the dress :
For these the manners, nay the mind, express :
That weight of wood, with leathern coat o'erlaid ;
Those ample clasps of solid metal made ;
The close-pressed leaves, unclosed for many an age ;
The dull red edging of the well-filled page ;
On the broad back the stubborn ridges rolled,
Where yet the title stands in tarnished gold ;
These all a sage and laboured work proclaim,
A painful candidate for lasting fame :

No idle wit, no trifling verse can lurk
In the deep bosom of that weighty work ;
No playful thoughts degrade the solemn style,
Nor one light sentence claims a transient smile.
　　Hence, in these times, untouched the pages lie,
And slumber out their immortality :
They *had* their day, when, after all his toil,
His morning study, and his midnight oil,
At length an author's ONE great work appeared,
By patient hope, and length of days endeared :
Expecting nations hailed it from the press ;
Poetic friends prefixed each kind address ;
Princes and kings received the pond'rous gift,
And ladies read the work they could not lift.
Fashion, though Folly's child, and guide of fools,
Rules e'en the wisest, and in learning rules ;
From crowds and courts to Wisdom's seat she goes,
And reigns triumphant o'er her mother's foes.
For lo ! these favourites of the ancient mode
Lie all neglected like the Birthday Ode.
　　Ah ! needless now this weight of massy chain,
Safe in themselves, the once-loved works remain ;
No readers now invade their still retreat,
None try to steal them from their parent seat ;
Like ancient beauties, they may now discard
Chains, bolts, and locks, and lie without a guard.
　　Our patient fathers trifling themes laid by,

And rolled, o'er laboured works, th' attentive eye :
Page after page the much enduring men
Explored the deeps and shallows of the pen :
Till, every former note and comment known,
They marked the spacious margin with their own ;
Minute corrections proved their studious care ;
The little index, pointing, told us where ;
And many an emendation showed the age
Looked far beyond the rubric title-page.

Our nicer palates lighter labours seek,
Cloyed with a folio-*Number* once a week ;
Bibles, with cuts and comments, thus go down :
E'en light Voltaire is *numbered* through the town :
Thus physic flies abroad, and thus the law,
From men of study, and from men of straw ;
Abstracts, abridgments, please the fickle times,
Pamphlets and plays, and politics and rhymes :
But though to write be now a task of ease,
The task is hard by manly arts to please,
When all our weakness is exposed to view,
And half our judges are our rivals too.

Amid these works, on which the eager eye
Delights to fix, or glides reluctant by,
When all combined, their decent pomp display,
Where shall we first our early offering pay ?—

To thee, DIVINITY ! to thee, the light
And guide of mortals, through their mental night ;

By whom we learn our hopes and fears to guide ;
To bear with pain, and to contend with pride ;
When grieved, to pray ; when injured, to forgive ;
And with the world in charity to live.

Not truths like these inspired that numerous race,
Whose pious labours fill this ample space ;
But questions nice, where doubt on doubt arose,
Awaked to war the long-contending foes.
For dubious meanings, learned polemics strove,
Aud wars on faith prevented works of love ;
The brands of discord far around were hurled,
And holy wrath inflamed a sinful world :—
Dull though impatient, peevish though devout,
With wit, disgusting, and despised without ;
Saints in design, in execution men,
Peace in their looks, and vengeance in their pen.

Methinks I see, and sicken at the sight,
Spirits of spleen from yonder pile alight ;
Spirits who prompted every damning page,
With pontiff pride, and still increasing rage :
Lo ! how they stretch their gloomy wings around,
And lash with furious strokes the trembling ground !
They pray, they fight, they murder, and they weep,
Wolves in their vengeance, in their manners sheep ;
Too well they act the prophet's fatal part,
Denouncing evil with a zealous heart ;
And each, like Jonah, is displeased if God

Repent his anger, or withhold his rod.
But here the dormant fury rests unsought,
And Zeal sleeps soundly by the foes she fought ;
Here all the rage of controversy ends,
And rival zealots rest like bosom friends :
An Athanasian here, in deep repose,
Sleeps with the fiercest of his Arian foes ;
Socinians here with Calvinists abide,
And thin partitions angry chiefs divide ;
Here wily Jesuits simple Quakers meet,
And Bellarmine has rest at Luther's feet.
Great authors, for the church's glory fired,
Are for the church's peace to rest retired ;
And close beside, a mystic, maudlin race,
Lie ' Crumbs of Comfort for the Babes of Grace.'
Against her foes Religion well defends
Her sacred truths, but often fears her friends ;
If learned, their pride, if weak, their zeal she dreads,
And their hearts' weakness, who have soundest heads.
But most she fears the controversial pen,
The holy strife of disputatious men ;
Who the blest Gospel's peaceful page explore,
Only to fight against its precepts more.
Near to these seats behold yon slender frames,
All closely filled and marked with modern names ;
Where no fair science ever shows her face,
Few sparks of genius, and no spark of grace ;

There sceptics rest, a still increasing throng,
And stretch their widening wings ten thousand strong ;
Some in close fight their dubious claims maintain ;
Some skirmish lightly, fly, and fight again ;
Coldly profane, and impiously gay,
Their end the same, though various in their way.
  When first Religion came to bless the land,
Her friends were then a firm believing band ;
To doubt was then to plunge in guilt extreme,
And all was gospel that a monk could dream ;
Insulted Reason fled the grov'lling soul,
For Fear to guide and visions to control :
But now, when Reason has assumed her throne,
She, in her turn demands to reign alone ;
Rejecting all that lies beyond her view,
And, being judge, will be a witness too :
Insulted Faith then leaves the doubtful mind,
To seek for truth, without a power to find :
Ah ! when will both in friendly beams unite,
And pour on erring man resistless light !
  Next to the seats, well stored with works divine,
An ample space, PHILOSOPHY ! is thine ;
Our reason's guide, by whose assisting light
We trace the moral bounds of wrong and right ;
Our guide through nature, from the sterile clay,
To the bright orbs of yon celestial way !
'Tis thine, the great, the golden chain to trace,

Which runs through all, connecting race with race,
Save where those puzzling, stubborn links remain,
Which thy inferior light pursues in vain :—
　　How vice and virtue in the soul contend ;
How widely differ, yet how nearly blend ;
What various passions war on either part,
And now confirm, now melt the yielding heart :
How Fancy loves around the world to stray,
While Judgment slowly picks his sober way ;
The stores of memory and the flights sublime
Of genius, bound by neither space nor time ;—
All these divine Philosophy explores,
Till, lost in awe, she wonders and adores.
　　From these, descending to the earth, she turns,
And matter, in its various forms, discerns ;
She parts the beamy light with skill profound,
Metes the thin air, and weighs the flying sound ;
'Tis hers the lightning from the clouds to call,
And teach the fiery mischief where to fall.
　　Yet more her volumes teach—on these we look
Abstracts drawn from Nature's larger book ;
Here, first described, the torpid earth appears,
And next, the vegetable robe it wears ;
Where flowery tribes in valleys, fields, and groves,
Nurse the still flame, and feed the silent loves ;
Loves where no grief, nor joy, nor bliss, nor pain,
Warm the glad heart or vex the labouring brain ;

But as the green blood moves along the blade,
The bed of Flora on the branch is made ;
Where, without passion, love instinctive lives,
And gives new life, unconscious that it gives.
Advancing still in Nature's maze, we trace,
In dens and burning plains, her savage race
With those tame tribes who on their lord attend,
And find in man a master and a friend ;
Man crowns the scene, a world of wonders new,
A moral world, that well demands our view.

This world is here ; for, of more lofty kind,
These neighbouring volumes reason on the mind ;
They paint the state of man ere yet endued
With knowledge ;—man, poor, ignorant, and rude ;
Then, as his state improves, their pages swell,
And all its cares, and all its comforts tell :
Here we behold how inexperience buys,
At little price, the wisdom of the wise ;
Without the troubles of an active state,
Without the cares and dangers of the great,
Without the miseries of the poor, we know
What wisdom, wealth, and poverty bestow ;
We see how reason calms the raging mind,
And how contending passions urge mankind :
Some, won by virtue, glow with sacred fire ;
Some, lured by vice, indulge the low desire ;
Whilst others, won by either, now pursue

The guilty chase, now keep the good in view ;
Forever wretched, with themselves at strife,
They lead a puzzled, vexed, uncertain life ;
For transient vice bequeaths a lingering pain,
Which transient virtue seeks to cure in vain.

Whilst thus engaged, high views enlarge the soul,
New interest draws, new principles control :
Nor thus the soul alone resigns her grief,
But here the tortured body finds relief ;
For see where yonder sage Arachnè shapes
Her subtle gin, that not a fly escapes !
There PHYSIC fills the space, and far around,
Pile above pile her learned works abound :
Glorious their aim—to ease the labouring heart ;
To war with death, and stop his flying dart ;
To trace the source whence the fierce contest grew ;
And life's short lease on easier terms renew ;
To calm the frenzy of the burning brain ;
To heal the tortures of imploring pain ;
Or, when more powerful ills all efforts brave,
To ease the victim no device can save,
And smooth the stormy passage to the grave.

But man, who knows no good unmixed and pure,
Oft finds a poison where he sought a cure ;
For grave deceivers lodge their labours here,
And cloud the science they pretend to clear ;
Scourges for sin, the solemn tribe are sent

Like fire and storms, they call us to repent ;
But storms subside, and fires forget to rage.
*These* are eternal scourges of the age :
'Tis not enough that each terrific hand
Spreads desolation round a guilty land ;
But trained to ill, and hardened by its crimes,
Their pen relentless kills through future times.
    Say, ye, who search these records of the dead—
Who read huge works, to boast what ye have read,
Can all the real knowledge ye possess,
Or those—if such there are—who more than guess,
Atone for each impostor's wild mistakes,
And mend the blunders pride or folly makes?
    What thought so wild, what airy dream so light,
That will not prompt a theorist to write?
What art so prevalent, what proofs so strong,
That will convince him his attempt is wrong?
One in the solids finds each lurking ill,
Nor grants the passive fluids power to kill ;
A learned friend some subtler reason brings,
Absolves the channels, but condemns their springs ;
The subtile nerves, that shun the doctor's eye,
Escape no more his subtler theory ;
The vital heat, that warms the labouring heart,
Lends a fair system to these sons of art ;
The vital air, a pure and subtile stream,
Serves a foundation for an airy scheme,

Assists the doctor and supports his dream.
Some have their favourite ills, and each disease
Is but a younger branch that kills from these ;
One to the gout contracts all human pain ;
He views it raging in the frantic brain ;
Finds it in fevers all his efforts mar,
And sees it lurking in the cold catarrh ;
Bilious by some, by others nervous seen,
Rage the fantastic demons of the spleen ;
And every symptom of the strange disease
With every system of the sage agrees.

Ye frigid tribe, on whom I wasted long
The tedious hours, and ne'er indulged in song ;
Ye first seducers of my easy heart,
Who promised knowledge ye could not impart ;
Ye dull deluders, truth's destructive foes ;
Ye sons of fiction, clad in stupid prose ;
Ye treacherous leaders, who, yourselves in doubt,
Light up false fires, and send us far about ;—
Still may yon spider round your pages spin,
Subtile and slow, her emblematic gin !
Buried in dust and lost in silence, dwell,
Most potent, grave, and reverend friends—farewell !

Near these, and where the setting sun displays,
Through the dim window, his departing rays,
And gilds yon columns, there, on either side,
The huge Abridgments of the Law abide ;

Fruitful as vice, the dread correctors stand,
And spread their guardian terrors round the land
Yet, as the best that human care can do
Is mixed with error, oft with evil too,
Skilled in deceit, and practised to evade,
Knaves stand secure, for whom these laws were made,
And justice vainly each expedient tries,
While art eludes it, or while power defies.
' Ah ! happy age,' the youthful poet sings,
' When the free nations knew not laws nor kings,
When all were blest to share a common store,
And none were proud of wealth, for none were poor,
No wars nor tumults vexed each still domain,
No thirst of empire, no desire of gain ;
No proud great man, nor one who would be great,
Drove modest merit from its proper state ;
Nor into distant climes would Avarice roam,
To fetch delights for Luxury at home :
Bound by no ties which kept the soul in awe,
They dwelt at liberty, and love was law ! '
    Mistaken youth ! each nation first was rude,
Each man a cheerless son of solitude,
To whom no joys of social life were known,
None felt a care that was not all his own ;
Or in some languid clime his abject soul
Bowed to a little tyrant's stern control ;
A slave, with slaves his monarch's throne he raised

And in rude song his ruder idol praised ;
The meaner cares of life were all he knew ;
Bounded his pleasures, and his wishes few ;
But when by slow degrees the Arts arose,
And Science wakened from her long repose ;
When Commerce, rising from the bed of ease,
Ran round the land, and pointed to the seas
When Emulation, born with jealous eye,
And Avarice, lent their spurs to industry ;
Then one by one the numerous laws were made,
Those to control, and these to succour trade ;
To curb the insolence of rude command,
To snatch the victim from the usurer's hand ;
To awe the bold, to yield the wronged redress,
And feed the poor with Luxury's excess.

Like some vast flood, unbounded, fierce, and strong,
His nature leads ungoverned man along ;
Like mighty bulwarks made to stem that tide,
The laws are formed and placed on every side ;
Whene'er it breaks the bounds by these decreed,
New statutes rise, and stronger laws succeed ;
More and more gentle grows the dying stream,
More and more strong the rising bulwarks seem ;
Till, like a miner working sure and slow,
Luxury creeps on, and ruins all below ;
The basis sinks, the ample piles decay ;
The stately fabric shakes and falls away ;

Primeval want and ignorance come on,
But Freedom, that exalts the savage state, is gone.
    Next HISTORY ranks ;—there full in front she lies,
And every nation her dread tale supplies ;
Yet History has her doubts, and every age
With sceptic queries marks the passing page ;
Records of old nor later date are clear,
Too distant those, and these are placed too near ;
There time conceals the objects from our view,
Here our own passions and a writer's too :
Yet, in these volumes, see how states arose !
Guarded by virtue from surrounding foes ;
Their virtue lost, and of their triumphs vain,
Lo ! how they sunk to slavery again !
Satiate with power, of fame and wealth possessed,
A nation grows too glorious to be blest ;
Conspicuous made, she stands the mark of all,
And foes join foes to triumph in her fall.
    Thus speaks the page that paints ambition's race,
The monarch's pride, his glory, his disgrace ;
The headlong course that maddening heroes run,
How soon triumphant, and how soon undone ;
How slaves, turned tyrants, offer crowns to sale,
And each fallen nation's melancholy tale.
    Lo ! where of late the Book of Martyrs stood,
Old pious tracts, and Bibles bound in wood ;
There, such the taste of our degenerate age,

Stand the profane delusions of the STAGE :
Yet virtue owns the TRAGIC MUSE a friend,
Fable her means, morality her end ;
For this she rules all passions in their turns,
And now the bosom bleeds, and now it burns ;
Pity with weeping eye surveys her bowl,
Her anger swells, her terror chills the soul ;
She makes the vile to virtue yield applause,
And own her sceptre while they break her laws ;
For vice in others is abhorred of all,
And villains triumph when the worthless fall.

   Not thus her sister COMEDY prevails,
Who shoots at Folly, for her arrow fails ;
Folly, by Dulness armed, eludes the wound,
And harmless sees the feathered shafts rebound ;
Unhurt she stands, applauds the archer's skill,
Laughs at her malice, and is Folly still.
Yet well the Muse portrays, in fancied scenes,
What pride will stoop to, what profession means ;
How formal fools the farce of state applaud ;
How caution watches at the lips of fraud ;
The wordy variance of domestic life ;
The tyrant husband, the retorting wife ;
The snares for innocence, the lie of trade,
And the smooth tongue's habitual masquerade.

   With her the Virtues to obtain a place,
Each gentle passion, each becoming grace ;

The social joy in life's securer road,
Its easy pleasure, its substantial good ;
The happy thought that conscious virtue gives,
And all that ought to live, and all that lives.

But who are these ?   Methinks a noble mien
And awful grandeur in their form are seen,
Now in disgrace : what though by time is spread
Polluting dust o'er every reverend head ;
What though beneath yon gilded tribe they lie,
And dull observers pass insulting by :
Forbid it shame, forbid it decent awe,
What seems so grave, should no attention draw !
Come, let us then with reverend step advance,
And greet—the ancient worthies of ROMANCE.

Hence, ye profane !   I feel a former dread,
A thousand visions float around my head :
Hark ! hollow blasts through empty courts resound,
And shadowy forms with staring eyes stalk round ;
See ! moats and bridges, walls and castles rise,
Ghosts, fairies, demons, dance before our eyes ;
Lo ! magic verse inscribed on golden gate ;
And bloody hand that beckons on to fate :—
' And who art thou, thou little page, unfold ?
Say, doth thy lord my Claribel withhold ?
Go tell him straight, Sir Knight, thou must resign
The captive queen ;—for Claribel is mine. '
Away he flies ; and now for bloody deeds,

Black suits of armour, masks, and foaming steeds ;
The giant falls ; his recreant throat I seize,
And from his corselet take the massy keys :—
Dukes, lords, and knights, in long procession move,
Released from bondage with my virgin love :—
She comes ! she comes ! in all the charms of youth,
Unequalled love, and unsuspected truth !

Ah, happy he who thus, in magic themes,
O'er worlds bewitched, in early rapture dreams,
Where wild Enchantment waves her potent wand,
And Fancy's beauties fill her fairy land ;
Where doubtful objects strange desires excite,
And Fear and Ignorance afford delight.

But lost, for ever lost, to me these joys,
Which Reason scatters, and which Time destroys ;
Too dearly bought : maturer judgment calls
My busied mind from tales and madrigals ;
My doughty giants all are slain or fled
And all my knights—blue, green, and yellow—dead !
No more the midnight fairy tribe I view,
All in the merry moonshine tippling dew ;
E'en the last lingering fiction of the brain,
The churchyard ghost is now at rest again ;
And all these wayward wanderings of my youth
Fly Reason's power, and shun the light of Truth.

With Fiction then does real joy reside,
And is our reason the delusive guide ?

Is it then right to dream the sirens sing ?
Or mount enraptured on the dragon's wing ?
No ; 'tis the infant mind, to care unknown,
That makes th' imagined paradise its own ;
Soon as reflections in the bosom rise,
Light slumbers vanish from the clouded eyes :
The tear and smile, that once together rose,
Are then divorced ; the head and heart are foes :
Enchantment bows to Wisdom's serious plan,
And Pain and Prudence make and mar the man.

While thus, of power and fancied empire vain,
With various thoughts my mind I entertain ;
While books, my slaves, with tyrant hand I seize,
Pleased with the pride that will not let them please,
Sudden I find terrific thoughts arise,
And sympathetic sorrow fills my eyes ;
For, lo ! while yet my heart admits the wound,
I see the CRITIC army ranged around.

Foes to our race ! if ever ye have known
A father's fears for offspring of your own ;
If ever, smiling o'er a lucky line,
Ye thought the sudden sentiment divine,
Then paused and doubted, and then, tired of doubt,
With rage as sudden dashed the stanza out ;—
If, after fearing much and pausing long,
Ye ventured on the world your laboured song,
And from the crusty critics of those days

Implored the feeble tribute of their praise ;
Remember now the fears that moved you then,
And, spite of truth, let mercy guide your pen.

What vent'rous race are ours ! what mighty foes
Lie waiting all around them to oppose !
What treacherous friends betray them to the fight !
What dangers threaten them :—yet still they write :
A hapless tribe ! to every evil born,
Whom villains hate, and fools affect to scorn :
Strangers they come, amid a world of woe,
And taste the largest portion ere they go.

Pensive I spoke, and cast mine eyes around ;
The roof, methought, returned a solemn sound ;
Each column seemed to shake, and clouds, like smoke,
From dusty piles and ancient volumes broke ;
Gathering above, like mists condensed they seem,
Exhaled in summer from the rushy stream ;
Like flowing robes they now appear, and twine
Round the large members of a form divine ;
His silver beard, that swept his aged breast,
His piercing eye, that inward light expressed,
Were seen—but clouds and darkness veiled the rest.
Fear chilled my heart : to one of mortal race,
How awful seemed the Genius of the place !
So in Cimmerian shores, Ulysses saw
His parent-shade, and shrunk in pious awe ;
Like him I stood, and wrapped in thought profound,

When from the pitying power broke forth a solemn
    sound :—
  ' Care lives with all ; no rules, no precepts save
The wise from woe, no fortitude the brave ;
Grief is to man as certain as the grave :
Tempests and storms in life's whole progress rise,
And hope shines dimly through o'erclouded skies.
Some drops of comfort on the favoured fall,
But showers of sorrow are the lot of *all* :
Partial to talents, then, shall Heaven withdraw
Th' afflicting rod, or break the general law ?
Shall he who soars, inspired by loftier views,
Life's little cares and little pains refuse ?
Shall he not rather feel a double share
Of mortal woe, when doubly armed to bear ?
  ' Hard is his fate who builds his peace of mind
On the precarious mercy of mankind ;
Who hopes for wild and visionary things,
And mounts o'er unknown seas with vent'rous wings ;
But as, of various evils that befall
The human race, some portion goes to all ;
To him perhaps the milder lot 's assigned
Who feels his consolation in his mind.
And, locked within his bosom, bears about
A mental charm for every care without.
E'en in the pangs of each domestic grief,
Or health or vigorous hope affords relief ;

And every wound the tortured bosom feels,
Or virtue bears, or some preserver heals;
Some generous friend of ample power possessed;
Some feeling heart, that bleeds for the distressed;
Some breast that glows with virtues all divine;
Some noble RUTLAND, misery's friend and thine.
  'Nor say, the Muse's song, the Poet's pen,
Merit the scorn they meet from little men.
With cautious freedom if the numbers flow,
Not wildly high, nor pitifully low;
If vice alone their honest aims oppose,
Why so ashamed their friends, so loud their foes?
Happy for men in every age and clime,
If all the sons of vision dealt in rhyme.
Go on, then, Son of Vision! still pursue
Thy airy dreams; the world is dreaming too.
Ambition's lofty views, the pomp of state,
The pride of wealth, the splendour of the great,
Stripped of their mask, their cares and troubles known,
Are visions far less happy than thy own;
Go on! and, while the sons of care complain,
Be wisely gay and innocently vain;
While serious souls are by their fears undone,
Blow sportive bladders in the beamy sun,
And call them worlds! and bid the greatest show
More radiant colours in their worlds below:
Then, as they break, the slaves of care reprove,
And tell them, Such are all the toys they love.'

## THE SOULS OF BOOKS.

EDWARD BULWER, LORD LYTTON.                *From 'Earlier Poems.'*

### I.

S IT here and muse !—it is an antique room—
    High-roof'd, with casements, through whose purple
      pane
Unwilling Daylight steals amidst the gloom,
Shy as a fearful stranger.
                There THEY reign
(In loftier pomp than waking life had known),
The Kings of Thought !—not crown'd until the grave.
When Agamemnon sinks into the tomb,
The beggar Homer mounts the Monarch's throne !
Ye ever-living and imperial Souls,
Who rule us from the page in which ye breathe,
All that divide us from the clod ye gave !—
Law—Order—Love—Intelligence—the Sense
Of Beauty—Music and the Minstrel's wreath !—
What were our wanderings if without your goals ?
As air and light, the glory ye dispense
Becomes our being—who of us can tell

What he had been, had Cadmus never taught
The art that fixes into form the thought—
Had Plato never spoken from his cell,
Or his high harp blind Homer never strung?
Kinder all earth hath grown since genial Shakspere sung !

## II.

Hark ! while we muse, without the walls is heard
The various murmur of the labouring crowd,
How still, within those archive-cells interr'd,
The Calm Ones reign !—and yet they rouse the loud
Passions and tumults of the circling world !
From them, how many a youthful Tully caught
The zest and ardour of the eager Bar ;
From them, how many a young Ambition sought
Gay meteors glancing o'er the sands afar—
By them each restless wing has been unfurl'd,
And their ghosts urge each rival's rushing car !
They made yon Preacher zealous for the truth ;
They made yon Poet wistful for the star ;
Gave Age its pastime—fired the cheek of Youth—
The unseen sires of all our beings are,—

## III.

And now so still ! This, Cicero, is thy heart ;
I hear it beating through each purple line.
This is thyself, Anacreon—yet, thou art

Wreath'd, as in Athens, with the Cnidian vine.
I ope thy pages, Milton, and, behold,
Thy spirit meets me in the haunted ground !—
Sublime and eloquent, as while, of old,
' It flamed and sparkled in its crystal bound ; ' [1]
These *are* yourselves—your life of life !   The Wise,
(Minstrel or Sage) *out* of their books are clay ;
But *in* their books, as from their graves, they rise,
Angels—that, side by side, upon our way,
Walk with and warn us !
                        Hark ! the world so loud,
And they, the movers of the world, so still !

What gives this beauty to the grave ?  the shroud
Scarce wraps the Poet, than at once there cease
Envy and Hate !   ' Nine cities claim him dead,
Through which the living Homer begg'd his bread ! '
And what the charm that can such health distil
From wither'd leaves—oft poisons in their bloom ?
We call some books immoral !   *Do they live ?*
If so, believe me, TIME hath made them pure.
In Books, the veriest wicked rest in peace—
God wills that nothing evil shall endure ;
The grosser parts fly off and leave the whole,
As the dust leaves the disembodied soul !
Come from thy niche, Lucretius !   Thou didst give
Man the black creed of Nothing in the tomb !

*Comus.*

Well, when we read thee, does the dogma taint?
No; with a listless eye we pass it o'er,
And linger only on the hues that paint
The Poet's spirit lovelier than his lore.
None learn from thee to cavil with their God;
None commune with thy genius to depart
Without a loftier instinct of the heart.
Thou mak'st no Atheist—thou but mak'st the mind
Richer in gifts which Atheists best confute—
FANCY AND THOUGHT!  'Tis these that from the sod
Lift us!  The life which soars above the brute
Ever and mightiest, breathes from a great Poet's lute!
Lo! that grim Merriment of Hatred;[1]—born
Of him,—the Master-Mocker of Mankind,
Beside the grin of whose malignant spleen,
Voltaire's gay sarcasm seems a smile serene,—
Do we not place it in our children's hands,
Leading young Hope through Lemuel's fabled lands?—
God's and man's libel in that foul Yahoo!—
Well, and what mischief can the libel do?
O impotence of Genius to belie
Its glorious task—its mission from the sky!
Swift wrote this book to wreak a ribald scorn
On aught the Man should love or Priest should mourn—
And lo! the book, from all its ends beguil'd,
A harmless wonder to some happy child!

*Gulliver's Travels.*

### IV.

All books grow homilies by time ; they are
Temples, at once, and Landmarks.   In them, we
Who *but* for them, upon that inch of ground
We call ' THE PRESENT,' from the cell could see
No daylight trembling on the dungeon bar ;
Turn, as we list, the globe's great axle round,
And feel the Near less household than the Far !
Traverse all space, and number every star,
There is no Past, so long as Books shall live !
A disinterr'd Pompeii wakes again
For him who seeks yon well ; lost cities give
Up their untarnish'd wonders, and the reign
Of Jove revives and Saturn :—at our will
Rise dome and tower on Delphi's sacred hill ;
Bloom Cimon's trees in Academe ; [1]—along
Leucadia's headland, sighs the Lesbian's song ;
With Ægypt's Queen once more we sail the Nile,
And learn how worlds are barter'd for a smile :—
Rise up, ye walls, with gardens blooming o'er,
Ope but that page—lo, Babylon once more !

### V.

Ye make the Past our  heritage and home :
And is this all ?   No ; by each prophet-sage—

[1] Plut. in *Vit. Cim.*

No ; by the herald souls that Greece and Rome
Sent forth, like hymns, to greet the Morning Star
That rose on Bethlehem,—by thy golden page,
Melodious Plato—by thy solemn dreams,
World-wearied Tully !—and, above ye all,
By THIS, the Everlasting Monument
Of God to mortals, on whose front the beams
Flash glory-breathing day—our lights ye are
To the dark Bourne beyond ; in you are sent
The types of Truths whose life is THE TO-COME ;
In you soars up the Adam from the fall ;
In you the FUTURE as the PAST is given—
Ev'n in our death ye bid us hail our birth ;—
Unfold these pages, and behold the Heaven,
Without one gravestone left upon the Earth ?

## *A FINAL WORD.*

### THE COLLECTOR TO HIS LIBRARY.

*Brown Books of mine, who never yet*
*Have caused me anguish or regret,—*
*Save when some fiend in human shape*
*Has set your tender sides agape,*
*Or soiled with some unmanly smear*
*The whiteness of your page sincere,*
*Or scored you with some phrase inane,*
*The bantling of his idle brain, —*
*I love you: and because must end*
*This commerce between friend and friend,*
*I do beseech each kindly fate—*
*To each and all I supplicate—*
*That you whom I have loved so long*
*May not be vended ' for a song,'—*
*That you, my dear desire and care,*
*May 'scape the common thoroughfare,*
*The dust, the eating rain, and all*
*The shame and squalor of the stall.*

*Rather I trust your lot may touch*
*Some Crœsus—if there should be such—*
*To buy you, and that you may so*
*From Crœsus unto Crœsus go*
*Till that inevitable day*
*When comes your moment of decay.*

*This, more than other good, I pray.*

AUSTIN DOBSON.